DK

POCKET
ENCYCLOPEDIA

FLOWER
ARRANGING

POCKET
ENCYCLOPEDIA

FLOWER
ARRANGING

Contributing editor
Malcolm Hillier

DORLING KINDERSLEY • LONDON

A Dorling Kindersley Book

First published in Great Britain in 1990
by Dorling Kindersley Limited,
9 Henrietta Street, London WC2E 8PS

Designed and edited by Swallow Books,
260 Pentonville Road, London N1 9JY

British Library Cataloguing in Publication Data

DK pocket encyclopedia, flower arranging
1. Flower arrangement
I. Hillier, Malcolm
745.92

ISBN 0-86318-434-0

Printed by Kyodo Printing Co (S'pore) Pte Ltd

CONTENTS

Introduction 6

INTRODUCTION

Flowers play an important part in our lives. Since the beginning of time they have been used to celebrate. Flowers are appropriate to so many occasions, so many different feelings and experiences. A simple bunch given to a friend or someone you love is magical. A decoration in the home for a special event makes an immensely personal statement. In times of happiness flowers can blaze with glory; in serenity, they can be tranquil, and in times of sadness they can bring solace. Their beauty can brighten the most ordinary of days. This book shows you how to introduce some of this beauty into your everyday life. It presents hundreds of inspirational ideas for fresh and dried flower arrangements to suit every occasion and every style of home. It also gives detailed advice on how to choose your flowers and foliage from the vast array of available plant material, and how to use them to create an arrangement for any occasion, simple or grand, formal or informal, summer or winter, and using fresh or dried flowers.

Flowers in the ancient world

The ancient Chinese attributed special meanings to the various plants that grew wild in the countryside and to those they cultivated. They used flowers in religious rituals and originally each arrangement contained only one type of flower. In the spring the paeony and peach blossom were most popular; the lotus epitomized summer, and the chrysanthemum, autumn. Plum blossom, white narcissus and pine branches were frequently used in winter.

In celebration of summer
An informal mixture of artemisia, Japanese anemones, delphiniums, everlasting sweet peas, spindle, blackberries, pearl everlasting, phlox, roses, montbretia, yarrow, euphorbia, veronica and globe amaranth.

The early Egyptians designed special vases for their flowers and often decorated the vases with floral motifs. The Greeks and Romans always incorporated flowers into their celebrations. They used leaves and flowers in their religious ceremonies, making headdresses, wreaths and garlands for bridal couples, and for heroes and athletes victorious in wars or games. Sometimes, for an assembly, they would strew a whole floor with scented rose petals.

The seventeenth and eighteenth centuries

In the West, the art of arranging flowers was first documented in the seventeenth century, when the Dutch, in particular, painted wonderful informal arrangements of flowers, foliage, fruit and vegetables. Such effects can be re-created today, using great mixtures of brilliantly colourful and scented flowers, combined with beautiful fruits, such as pineapples, pomegranates, mulberries and crab apples, and garden vegetables with interesting shapes, like curly kale, cabbage, beans or peppers.

In the eighteenth century, many potteries produced vases for flowers as well as china for the table. Wedgwood and Sèvres are the best known makers of ceramic flower containers during this period. Arrangements were used to decorate the houses of wealthy families and the aristocracy on a regular basis. Vases of flowers sat on the newly introduced mantelshelves, and in summer a vase of flowers was sited in the fireplace, standing on the hearth. Arrangements were also placed on tables, which were brought into the body of the room.

In Britain, the most popular flowers in summer were roses, carnations, irises, paeonies, delphiniums, monkshood and hollyhocks. Although

Historical pastiche
An arrangement in seventeenth-century Flemish style, using flowers from different seasons, including lilies, amaryllis, irises, eucomis, hollyhocks, hydrangea, vine, delphiniums, carnations, tulips, tobacco plant, everlasting peas, chicory, roses, nerines, poppies, peaches and pomegranate.

the chrysanthemum was introduced from China to the West at this time, it was not until a century later that it became a popular flower, and was used to decorate the house in all manner of flower arrangements.

Contrasting colours
This cool mixture of blue cornflowers, straw-yellow helichrysum heads and feathery, silvery acacia foliage harmonizes beautifully with the early Delft flower-patterned bowl.

The nineteenth century

The Victorians retained informality in their arrangements, resulting in some very beautiful, romantic creations in the manner of those painted by Fantin Latour. They used tremendous mixtures of flowers: it was during the nineteenth century that the majority of plant introductions took place and the Victorians were great hybridizers.

They brought to England and the United States many plants from China, Africa and South America. Some of them – like rhododendrons, azaleas, tree paeonies, roses and gladioli – have become favourite garden plants. Others – like begonias, calceolarias and fuchsias – were grown under glass and bedded out for the summer months. Plants like carnations and auriculas were developed in their thousands to produce very fancy striped and blotched varieties.

Roses were crossed to produce fabulous blooms with a great number of petals, and most of them were wonderfully scented as well.

But fond as Victorian ladies were of tremendous mixtures of flowers, equally frequently they placed a single type of flower in a vase, either alone or with a few stems of interesting foliage, such as ferns, grasses or bulrushes. It was at this time that striking colour contrasts were employed for the first time, and many of these schemes are still in use today.

In the second half of the nineteenth century many books were published on the subject of flower arranging. They contained illustrations of elaborate, wild decorations for dinner parties and special seasonal occasions, including wonderful garlands and swags, and many-tiered epergnes, or ornamental centrepieces, for sideboards or dinner tables. Even Mrs Beeton's *Household Management* includes mention of flower arrangement.

Interest in flower arranging was also developing apace in the United States, where brighter colours and new flower shapes were becoming available, such as dahlias and nasturtiums, azaleas and camellias. At a time when there were few leisure occupations open for women outside the home, women's magazines contained plenty of advice on looking after and displaying cut flowers. It soon became the norm to have arrangements placed in every room.

At the end of the century arrangements became subjects for the Impressionist painters, from Van Gogh with his "Sunflowers" and Bonnard, with a bombardment of rich colour, to Manet and Monet. They portrayed flowers in a quite different way, suggesting the scent, colour and mood of arrangements rather than painting realistic representations.

Following the seasons
The Flemish and Italian artists of the seventeenth century used artistic licence to fill their vases with a myriad flowers from every season, but today we can

do nearly as well in reality, as more and more flowers become available all year.

Flower shops carry not only seasonal flowers but many beautiful and exotic blooms from around the world. Keeping your arrangements seasonal, however, is the way to achieve the most natural-looking results. Early summer is the very best time of year for flowers. Colours are both at their richest and most subtle: reds and blues, peaches, apricots and creams, deep and pale yellows are all offset by the brilliant greens of fresh foliage. Summer is also the time of silver, lilac and pink.

The colours of bonfires and the setting sun are the colours of autumn flowers. In early and mid-winter flowers are very scarce. But popping up in the gloom are winter jasmine, the Christmas rose, winter cherry, some of the viburnums and mahonia. Suddenly the greyness begins to lift and soon yellows and white abound, and to echo the spring skies there are touches of clear blue in hyacinth, scilla and iris.

The history of dried flowers

While there is a precious quality about the impermanence of fresh flowers, it is exciting to know that the pleasure they bring can be prolonged. Nearly every plant can be dried or preserved.

When certain flowers and leaves are dried they retain their perfume and these have been used for centuries, both to adorn and perfume rooms. In the seventeenth century posies of aromatic and scented plants, often dried, were carried to ward off plague.

In the nineteenth century the imagination of the Victorians was captured by their great plant hunters. Enthusiasts at home made wonderful collections of pressed flowers and leaves and arrangements of dried flowers, grasses and rushes. Then interest in dried flowers gradually waned until by the early 1970s the selection available in shops was limited to just a few grasses, statice and strawflowers, often dyed in violent colours.

Border garden
(opposite)
With a large garden you can afford the luxury of wide mixed borders. At the beginning of summer, these borders will yield plentiful yellow and white achillea, delphiniums, and alchemilla.

The revival of interest

About fifteen years ago leading flower arrangers
began experimenting with the air drying of blooms
and leaves. They found that they could preserve a
much greater range of natural colours in the more
usual drying flowers than was available ready dried,
and they went on to establish a regular supply of
roses, delphiniums, larkspur, astilbe, gypsophila and
mimosa along with a host of other flowers, grasses,
seed-heads and leaves.

The list of flowers expanded year after year, and
with it an interest was awakened that has now made
dried flowers a growth industry. Commercial
nurseries all over the world are growing flowers
solely for drying, and it is now possible to buy ready-
dried flowers native to many distant countries.

Drying techniques

Although air drying is the simplest and most effective
method, there are several other ways that plant
material can be preserved. Chemical dessicants and
sand can be used to draw the moisture from plant
material to provide very beautiful, but brittle flowers
that keep much of their colour and texture. Glycerine
can replace the moisture content of many leaves and
some flowers, so retaining suppleness but often
altering colours. Pressing plant material between
sheets of absorbent paper is a method of drying that
keeps colours true but flattens the material, making it
more suitable for mounting under glass. All these
techniques are explained in detail in the book.

Overhead view
(above)
*This wicker basket is
crammed full of field
grasses interlaced with
yellow helichrysum,
anaphalis, helipterum,
achillea and silene.*

The flower arranger's garden

If you are fortunate enough to have a garden, it is
relatively easy to grow plants that you can harvest
and arrange, while fresh or after drying yourself.
Undertaking the whole process of growing,
preserving and arranging is a rewarding experience.
It is as exciting to dry a few mixed bunches as it is to
fill a whole ceiling space with material you have

grown. Even in a small garden of 6 × 9 m
(20 × 30 ft), you can grow enough material to make
three or four large dried-flower arrangements
without greatly affecting the look of the garden.

That flowers for drying have to be picked just
before they reach perfection is an important point
when planning your garden. A border should be
planted so that it will not be denuded as soon as
flowers and foliage are harvested for drying. The
currently popular mixed border, which contains
herbaceous perennials, shrubs, climbers, roses and
annuals, is the ideal site for a good selection of plants
for drying. However, many rushes and ferns, which
provide the fronds, stems and seed-heads that are
essential to many dried-flower arrangements, tend to
prefer very damp soil and are therefore best grown in
a separate area of the garden.

The secrets of arranging flowers

The exciting processes of growing and drying
flowers, or simply buying bunches of fresh or dried
flowers, are merely preliminaries to the creative art
of arranging them.

This book will help to demonstrate the techniques
that lead to making an arrangement. However, it
has to be said that there are no rules for arranging
flowers, no lists of fresh or dried flowers that look
nice together, no definitive combinations of colours
that work better than others. The best advice must
be to look to nature for your lead when creating
with flowers.

This book shows you the wide range of plant
material that can be grown and dried and presents
some of the ways this material can be arranged,
frequently taking inspiration from the way that plants
grow and the shapes they make in the landscape.
Some of the arrangements are simple, whereas those
for special occasions are more complex. Everyone
needs a little inspiration to develop creativity: this
book will provide you with just that.

Accent on scent
*Of all the freesias, the
coloured single flowers
have the very best clear,
sweet perfume.*

FRESH
FLOWERS

———

CHAPTER ONE

GUIDE TO FRESH FLOWERS AND FOLIAGE

During the course of the year we are provided with an enormous wealth of plant material. At the end of winter, there is that magic moment when the first crocuses and daffodils appear. Suddenly the fields and hedgerows come alive with flowers and foliage, the colour yellow predominating. In summer the colour range changes, with plenty of pink, red and blue flowers and occasional patches of yellow.

Autumn throws up more mellow colours: rusts, reds, ambers, golds and oranges dominate the borders, although there are still some pale pinks, creams and white around. In winter there are fewer flowers and we have to rely more on the dark greens of evergreen foliage and the reds of winter berries.

Summer fragrance
The early summer sun warms this basket filled with the loveliest of fresh flowers – delphiniums, paeonies, spurge, sweet peas, bridal wreath, whitebeam, cow parsley and corn marigolds. The heady fragrance of the paeonies and sweet peas heightens the sensual pleasure.

Spring flowers

White dead nettle
Lamium album

Rosemary
Rosmarinus officinalis

Forsythia
Forsythia × *intermedia*

Sweet violet
Viola odorata

Orchid
Cymbidium hybrid

Borage
Borago officinalis

Forget-me-not
Myosotis alpestris

Spiraea
Spiraea thunbergii

Jew's mallow
Kerria japonica 'Pleniflora'

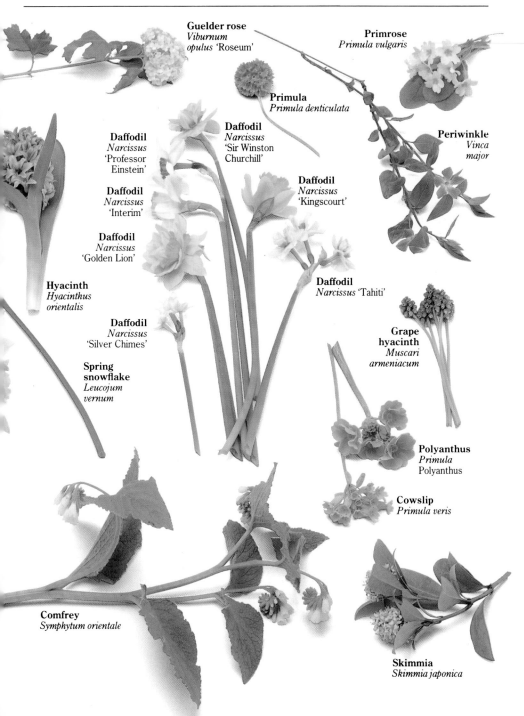

Guelder rose
*Viburnum
opulus* 'Roseum'

Primrose
Primula vulgaris

Primula
Primula denticulata

Periwinkle
*Vinca
major*

Daffodil
Narcissus
'Professor
Einstein'

Daffodil
Narcissus
'Sir Winston
Churchill'

Daffodil
Narcissus
'Kingscourt'

Daffodil
Narcissus
'Interim'

Daffodil
Narcissus
'Golden Lion'

Daffodil
Narcissus 'Tahiti'

Hyacinth
*Hyacinthus
orientalis*

Daffodil
Narcissus
'Silver Chimes'

**Grape
hyacinth**
*Muscari
armeniacum*

**Spring
snowflake**
*Leucojum
vernum*

Polyanthus
Primula
Polyanthus

Cowslip
Primula veris

Comfrey
Symphytum orientale

Skimmia
Skimmia japonica

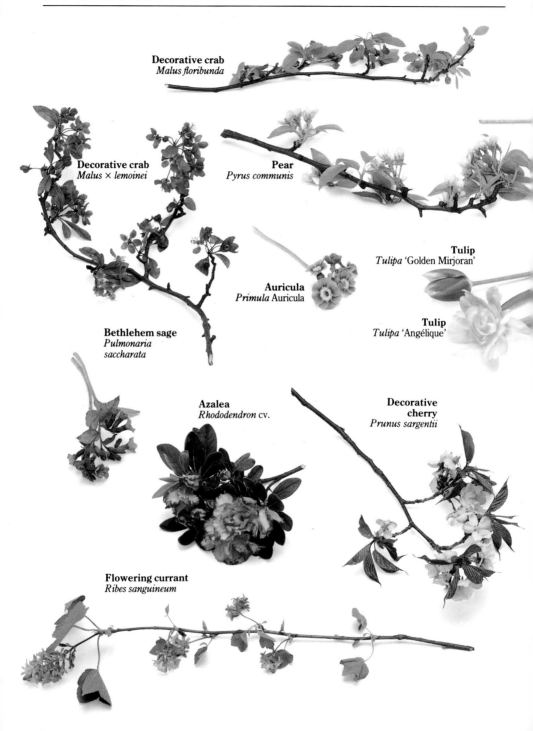

Decorative crab
Malus floribunda

Decorative crab
Malus × lemoinei

Pear
Pyrus communis

Auricula
Primula Auricula

Tulip
Tulipa 'Golden Mirjoran'

Tulip
Tulipa 'Angélique'

Bethlehem sage
*Pulmonaria
saccharata*

Azalea
Rhododendron cv.

**Decorative
cherry**
Prunus sargentii

Flowering currant
Ribes sanguineum

Anemone
Anemone coronaria
'The Bride'

Flowering quince
Chaenomeles speciosa

Wallflower
Cheiranthus cheiri

Lilac
Syringa vulgaris 'Mme
Florent Stepman'

Camellia
*Camellia
japonica*

Pansy
Viola × wittrockiana

Tulip
Tulipa 'Estella
Rijnveld'

Viburnum
Viburnum carlesii 'Aurora'

Lenten rose
*Helleborus
orientalis*

Magnolia
Magnolia kobus

Pasqueflower
Pulsatilla vulgaris

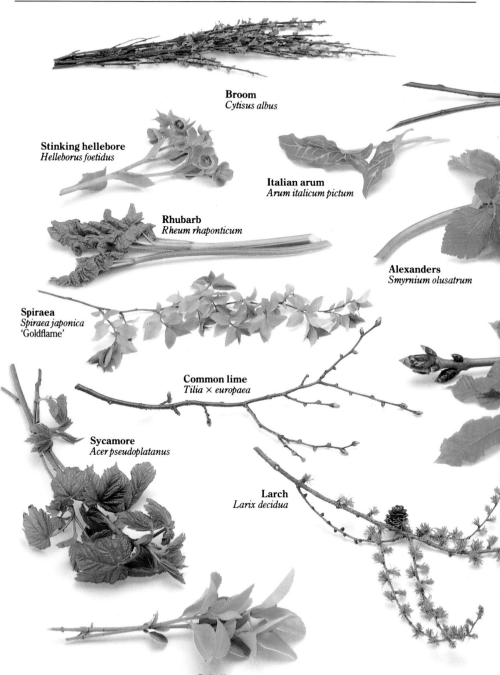

Broom
Cytisus albus

Stinking hellebore
Helleborus foetidus

Italian arum
Arum italicum pictum

Rhubarb
Rheum rhaponticum

Alexanders
Smyrnium olusatrum

Spiraea
Spiraea japonica
'Goldflame'

Common lime
Tilia × europaea

Sycamore
Acer pseudoplatanus

Larch
Larix decidua

Spindle
Euonymus japonicus aureus

Honeysuckle
Lonicera periclymenum 'Belgica'

Fig
Ficus carica

Hornbeam
Carpinus betulus

Horse chestnut
Aesculus hippocastanum

Pussy willow
Salix caprea

Mrs Robb's bonnet
*Euphorbia amygdaloides
robbiae*

Lilac
Syringa vulgaris

Summer flowers

Ceanothus
Ceanothus impressus

Columbine
Aquilegia

Candytuft
Iberis

Chives
*Allium
schoenoprasum*

Laburnum
*Laburnum
× watereri* 'Vossii'

**Bleeding
heart**
*Dicentra
spectabilis*

Ranunculus
*Ranunculus
asiaticus*

Clematis
Clematis 'Nellie
Moser'

Snakeweed
Polygonum bistorta

Thrift
Armeria plantaginea

Wood spurge
*Euphorbia
amygdaloides*

Alkanet
Pentaglottis sempervirens

Whitebeam
Sorbus aria
'Lutescens'

Broom
Cytisus × praecox

Jacob's ladder
Polemonium foliosissimum

Cow parsley
Anthriscus sylvestris

Iris
Iris cv.

Lily-of-the-valley
Convallaria majalis

Spanish bluebell
Hyacinthoides campanulatus

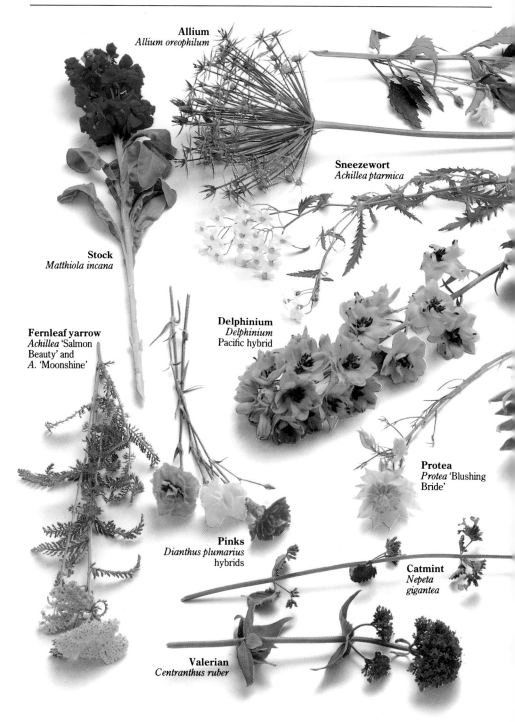

Allium
Allium oreophilum

Sneezewort
Achillea ptarmica

Stock
Matthiola incana

Fernleaf yarrow
Achillea 'Salmon
Beauty' and
A. 'Moonshine'

Delphinium
Delphinium
Pacific hybrid

Protea
Protea 'Blushing
Bride'

Pinks
Dianthus plumarius
hybrids

Catmint
*Nepeta
gigantea*

Valerian
Centranthus ruber

Bellflower
Campanula trachelium
'Alba Plena'

Lupin
Lupinus Russell
strain

Lily
Lilium
regale

Rose
Rosa 'Golden
Wings'

Cherry
Prunus avium
'Early Rivers'

Protea
Protea
obtusifolia

Cornflower
Centaurea
cyanus

Asparagus
Asparagus
officinalis

Sweet William
Dianthus barbatus

Snapdragon
Antirrhinum majus

Sweet pea
Lathyrus odoratus

Pink rose
Rosa cv.

Yellow rose
Rosa
'Courvoisier'

Lilac rose
Rosa 'Variegata
di Bologna'

Masterwort
Astrantia major

**Yellow horned-
poppy**
Glaucium flavum

Astilbe
Astilbe
× *arendsii*

Shasta daisy
*Leucanthemum
maximum*

Foxglove
Digitalis purpurea

Allium
Allium aflatunense

Rose
Rosa 'Charles de Mills'

Mock orange
Philadelphus 'Burfordensis'

White paeony
Paeonia lactiflora 'Festiva Maxima'

Pink paeony
Paeonia lactiflora cv.

Brodiaea
Brodiaea laxa

Love-in-a-mist
Nigella damascena

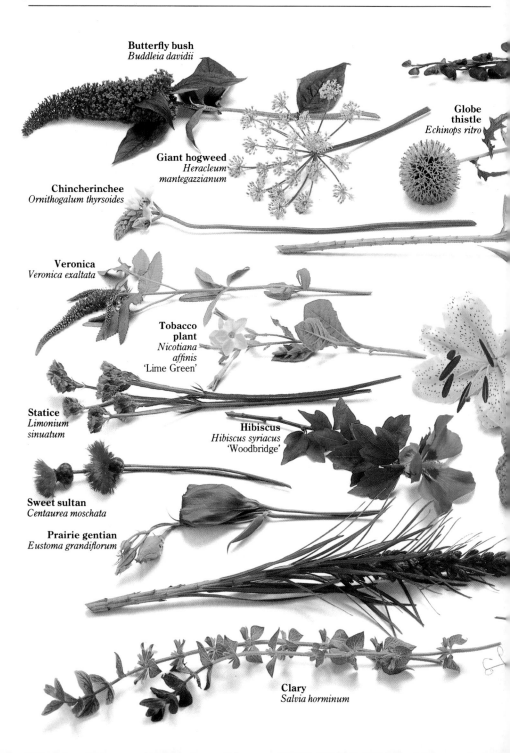

Butterfly bush
Buddleia davidii

Globe thistle
Echinops ritro

Giant hogweed
Heracleum mantegazzianum

Chincherinchee
Ornithogalum thyrsoides

Veronica
Veronica exaltata

Tobacco plant
Nicotiana affinis
'Lime Green'

Statice
Limonium sinuatum

Hibiscus
Hibiscus syriacus
'Woodbridge'

Sweet sultan
Centaurea moschata

Prairie gentian
Eustoma grandiflorum

Clary
Salvia horminum

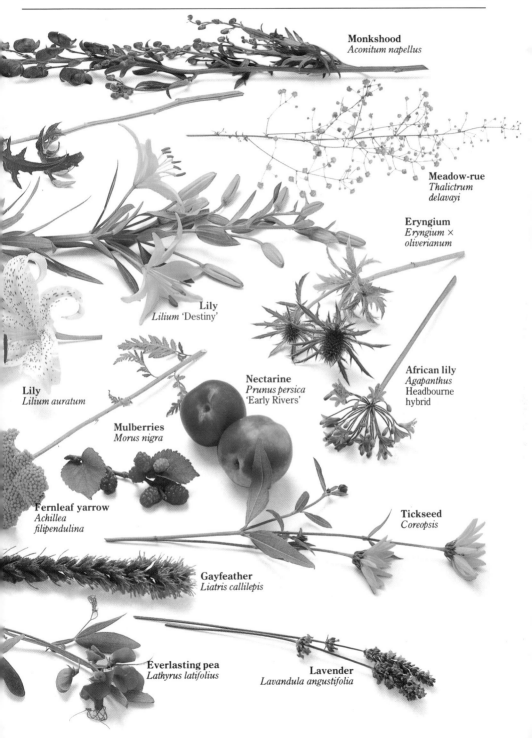

Monkshood
Aconitum napellus

Meadow-rue
Thalictrum delavayi

Eryngium
Eryngium × oliverianum

Lily
Lilium 'Destiny'

African lily
Agapanthus Headbourne hybrid

Lily
Lilium auratum

Nectarine
Prunus persica 'Early Rivers'

Mulberries
Morus nigra

Fernleaf yarrow
Achillea filipendulina

Tickseed
Coreopsis

Gayfeather
Liatris callilepis

Everlasting pea
Lathyrus latifolius

Lavender
Lavandula angustifolia

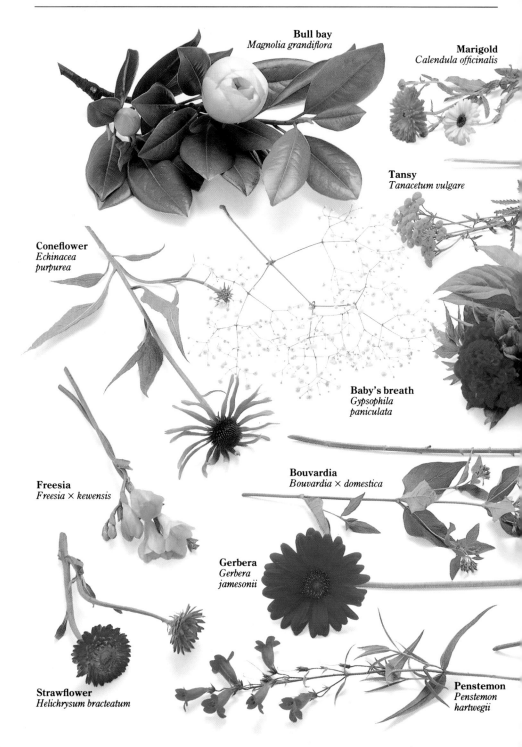

Bull bay
Magnolia grandiflora

Marigold
Calendula officinalis

Tansy
Tanacetum vulgare

Coneflower
*Echinacea
purpurea*

Baby's breath
*Gypsophila
paniculata*

Freesia
Freesia × kewensis

Bouvardia
Bouvardia × domestica

Gerbera
*Gerbera
jamesonii*

Strawflower
Helichrysum bracteatum

Penstemon
*Penstemon
hartwegii*

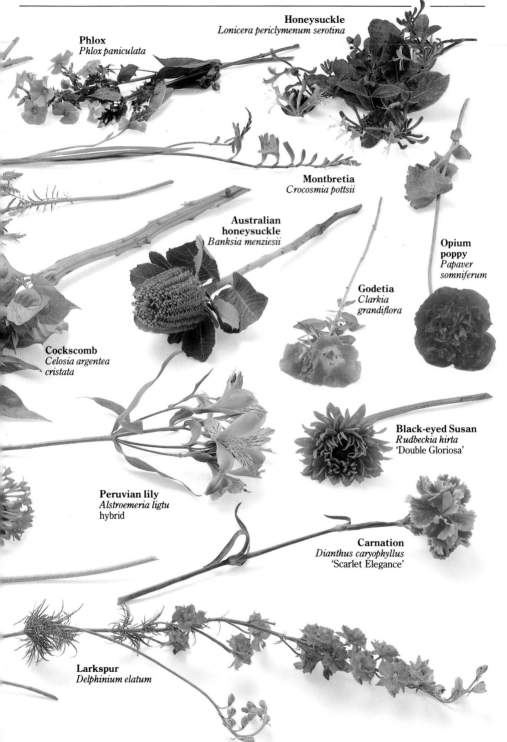

Honeysuckle
Lonicera periclymenum serotina

Phlox
Phlox paniculata

Montbretia
Crocosmia pottsii

**Australian
honeysuckle**
Banksia menziesii

**Opium
poppy**
*Papaver
somniferum*

Godetia
*Clarkia
grandiflora*

Cockscomb
*Celosia argentea
cristata*

Black-eyed Susan
Rudbeckia hirta
'Double Gloriosa'

Peruvian lily
Alstroemeria ligtu
hybrid

Carnation
Dianthus caryophyllus
'Scarlet Elegance'

Larkspur
Delphinium elatum

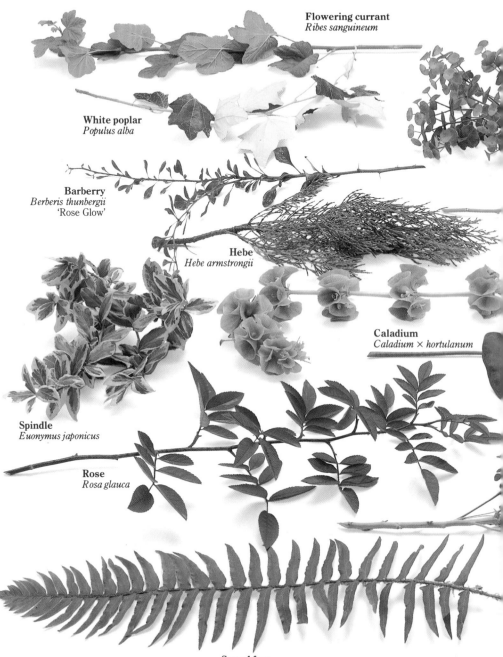

Flowering currant
Ribes sanguineum

White poplar
Populus alba

Barberry
Berberis thunbergii
'Rose Glow'

Hebe
Hebe armstrongii

Caladium
Caladium × hortulanum

Spindle
Euonymus japonicus

Rose
Rosa glauca

Sword fern
Nephrolepsis exaltata

Artemisia
Artemisia ludoviciana

Cotton lavender
Santolina chamaecyparissus

Wood spurge
Euphorbia amygdaloides

Senecio
Senecio 'Sunshine'

Plantain lily
Hosta fortunei
'Aureomarginata'

Jew's mallow
Kerria japonica ·

**Bells of
Ireland**
*Moluccella
laevis*

Fig
Ficus carica

Lamb's tongue
Stachys byzantina

Rue
Ruta graveolens

Lady's mantle
Alchemilla mollis

Dogwood
Cornus alba
'Elegantissima'

Autumn flowers

Acidanthera
Gladiolus callianthus

Strawberry tree
Arbutus unedo

Corn-on-the-cob
Zea mays

Michaelmas daisy
Aster ericoides
'Monte Casino'

Chrysanthemum
Chrysanthemum
'Statesman'

Chrysanthemum
Chrysanthemum
'Evelyn Bush'

Bouvardia
Bouvardia × domestica

Rose of Sharon
Hypericum calycinum

Milkweed
Gomphocarpus

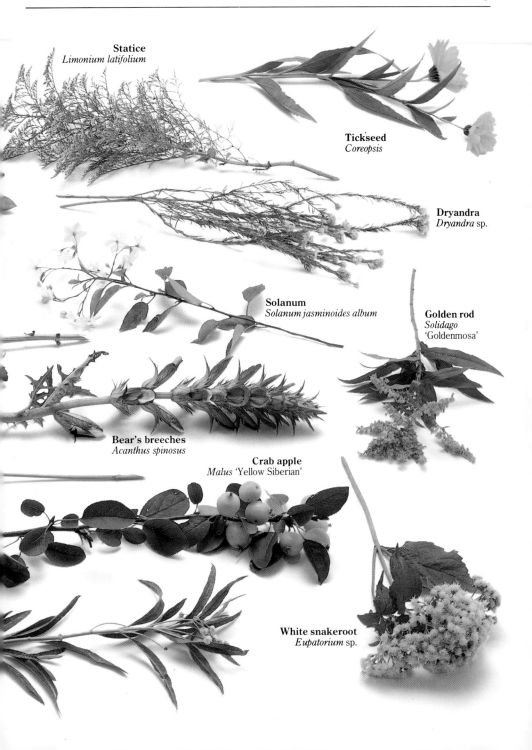

Statice
Limonium latifolium

Tickseed
Coreopsis

Dryandra
Dryandra sp.

Solanum
Solanum jasminoides album

Golden rod
Solidago
'Goldenmosa'

Bear's breeches
Acanthus spinosus

Crab apple
Malus 'Yellow Siberian'

White snakeroot
Eupatorium sp.

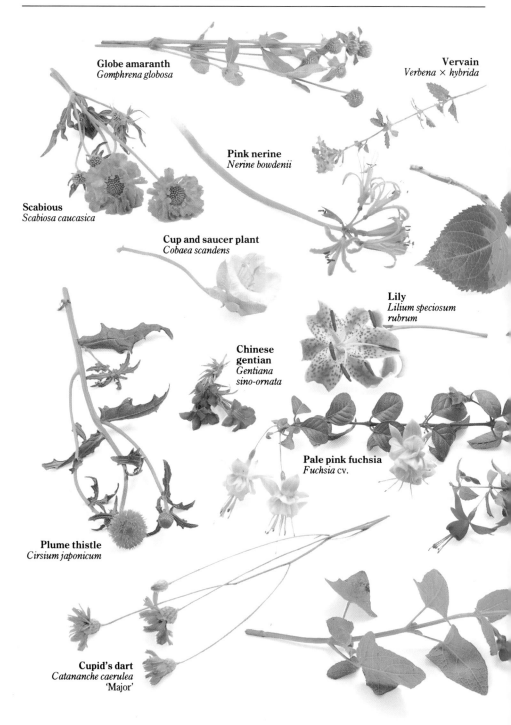

Globe amaranth
Gomphrena globosa

Vervain
Verbena × hybrida

Pink nerine
Nerine bowdenii

Scabious
Scabiosa caucasica

Cup and saucer plant
Cobaea scandens

Lily
*Lilium speciosum
rubrum*

**Chinese
gentian**
*Gentiana
sino-ornata*

Pale pink fuchsia
Fuchsia cv.

Plume thistle
Cirsium japonicum

Cupid's dart
Catananche caerulea
'Major'

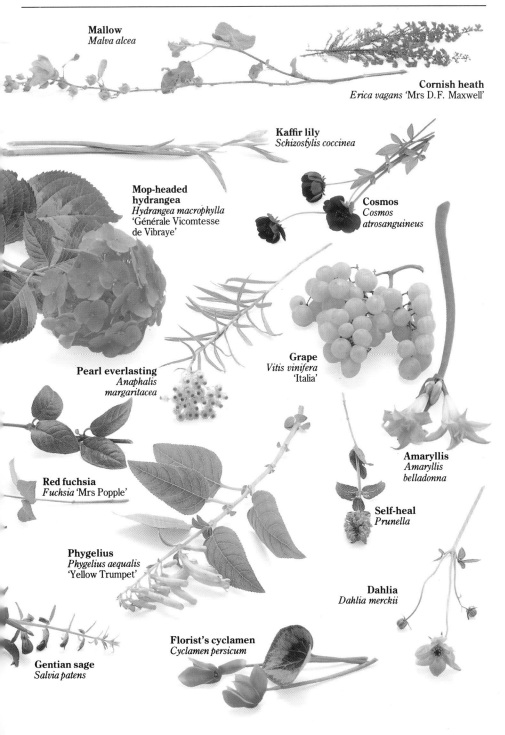

Mallow
Malva alcea

Cornish heath
Erica vagans 'Mrs D.F. Maxwell'

Kaffir lily
Schizostylis coccinea

**Mop-headed
hydrangea**
Hydrangea macrophylla
'Générale Vicomtesse
de Vibraye'

Cosmos
*Cosmos
atrosanguineus*

Pearl everlasting
*Anaphalis
margaritacea*

Grape
Vitis vinifera
'Italia'

Amaryllis
*Amaryllis
belladonna*

Red fuchsia
Fuchsia 'Mrs Popple'

Self-heal
Prunella

Phygelius
Phygelius aequalis
'Yellow Trumpet'

Dahlia
Dahlia merckii

Florist's cyclamen
Cyclamen persicum

Gentian sage
Salvia patens

Love-lies-bleeding
Amaranthus caudatus

Waratah
Telopea sp.

Chrysanthemum
Chrysanthemum indicum

Dahlia
Dahlia
'Nina Chester'

Pepper
*Capsicum annuum
acuminatum*
'Friesdorfer'

Chrysanthemum
Chrysanthemum
'Mason's Bronze'

Michaelmas daisy
Aster novae-angliae

Chrysanthemum
*Chrysanthemum
indicum*
'Charming'

Chinese lantern
*Physalis alkekengi
franchetii*

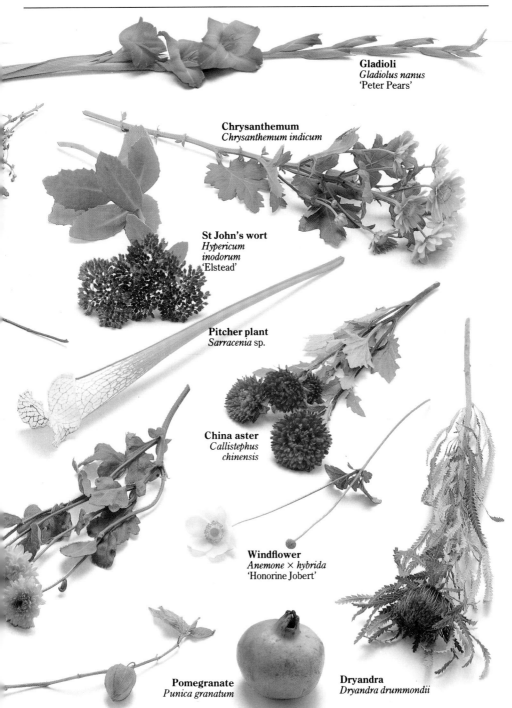

Gladioli
Gladiolus nanus
'Peter Pears'

Chrysanthemum
Chrysanthemum indicum

St John's wort
*Hypericum
inodorum*
'Elstead'

Pitcher plant
Sarracenia sp.

China aster
*Callistephus
chinensis*

Windflower
Anemone × *hybrida*
'Honorine Jobert'

Pomegranate
Punica granatum

Dryandra
Dryandra drummondii

Snowdrop tree
Halesia monticola

Guelder rose
Viburnum opulus

Horse chestnut
Aesculus sp.

Firethorn
Pyracantha coccinea
'Lalandei'

Stranvaesia
Photinia davidiana

Berberis
Berberis thunbergii
atropurpurea

Rose hips
Rosa cv.

Forsythia
*Forsythia ×
intermedia*

Spindle
Euonymus europaeus

Sweet briar
Rosa eglanteria

Crab apple
*Malus ×
lemoinei*

Strawberry tree
Arbutus unedo

Tulip tree
*Liriodendron
tulipifera*

Sweet gum
*Liquidambar
styraciflua*

Crab apple
Malus 'Profusion'

Scarlet oak
Quercus coccinea

Winter flowers

Daphne
Daphne odora

Silk tassel bush
Garrya elliptica

Heather
Erica × darleyensis
'Darley Dale'

Euphorbia
Euphorbia fulgens

Wintersweet
Chimonanthus praecox

Primula
Primula obconica

Viburnum
Viburnum × bodnantense

Snowdrop
Galanthus nivalis

Winter aconite
Eranthis hyemalis

Witch hazel
Hamamelis mollis

Winter heliotrope
Petasites fragrans

Honeysuckle
Lonicera × purpusii

Poinsettia
Euphorbia pulcherrima

Laurustinus
Viburnum tinus

Mahonia
Mahonia × media 'Charity'

Hellebore
Helleborus argutifolius

Iris
Iris danfordiae

Iris
Iris unguicularis

Winter jasmine
Jasminum nudiflorum

Elaeagnus
Elaeagnus pungens 'Maculata'

Griselinia
Griselinia littoralis

Hemlock
Tsuga canadensis

Yew
Taxus baccata

Cotoneaster
Cotoneaster 'Cornubia'

Camellia
Camellia japonica

Shallon
Gaultheria shallon

Mahonia
Mahonia × media 'Charity'

Skimmia
Skimmia japonica

Mrs Robb's bonnet
Euphorbia amygdaloides robbiae

Senecio
Senecio 'Sunshine'

Portugal laurel
Prunus lusitanica

Southern beech
Nothofagus betuloides

Blue spruce
Picea pungens glauca

Holly
Ilex aquifolium

Parchment-bark
Pittosporum tobira
'Variegatum'

Ivy
Hedera helix

Rosemary
Rosmarinus officinalis

Fatsia
Fatsia japonica

Lawson's cypress
Chamaecyparis
lawsoniana 'Lutea'

· CHAPTER TWO ·

PRINCIPLES OF FRESH FLOWER ARRANGING

There is no need to find the thought of creating an arrangement of fresh flowers daunting. Although there are no hard and fast rules about what will look attractive, there are some guidelines that you may find useful. Whichever type of arrangement you wish to make, it is simply a matter of choosing a group of flower shapes and foliage that go well together, and whose colours work with the style and the decoration of the room in which the arrangement will be placed. The scale of an arrangement is important too, especially if it is to be seen by a large group of people. Choose a container that will complement both flowers and foliage, and the room, and, lastly, consider the scent of the plant material you plan to use.

These factors are not nearly as restricting as they may at first sound. Flowers are so beautiful that almost any combination of forms and colours is bound to look attractive.

Complementary container
An abundant arrangement in a blue and white faïence cachepot stands before a doorway into the courtyard of Ightham Mote in Kent, England. The delphiniums pick up the blue of the design amidst a sea of white dill, pale green maidenhair fern, a sprinkling of yellow alstroemeria and the stems of tea tree.

Style

Before starting to create an arrangement of flowers, think about where you want to position it and how it will relate to the designs, colours, forms and textures around it. Consider the space that will surround the arrangement and how that space is used. This will give you an idea of the scale and size it should be.

If it is to stand on a hallway table, then it must be large enough to be noticed, but it must not be so wide that it obstructs people walking through the hall.

If the arrangement is to go on a dining table, then it must look attractive from the points of view of all the diners, and it must not take up too much of the table, making the place settings or serving areas cramped. Most importantly, it must not obstruct the view of the guests. This does not mean that it cannot be tall, but if it is tall it must be narrow, with the flowers held above eye level.

If it is for a bedside table, then leave space for a book and for leaning across to check the time or turn off the alarm.

Low arrangement for a coffee table
The contrast between the pink of the Attila tulips and the blue of the flower bowl gives this low arrangement dramatic interest. The stems have been cut short to keep the tulips compact and bushy.

An arrangement for a coffee table should look good from above and every side. It should not take up too much room: you may want to place coffee cups on the table after dinner. A shelf arrangement should not look cramped beneath the shelf above it. Remember that in any situation, the flowers should always have space to declare themselves attractively. An arrangement for a fireplace rarely looks good fitted into the grate of the fire. It is much better to stand it on the hearth in front of the grate. Remember that it will probably be seen from the sides as well as the front.

Matching the decorations

Always take into account the atmosphere of the room. Chrome and modern glass rarely look attractive in a Victorian or chintzy setting, whereas they can look very special against old well-patinated wood, such as oak, as well as in a modern room. If the decorations are sombre, rich-coloured flowers and containers look best. In a pastel room, pale-coloured flowers, with touches of bright colour, are ideal.

Although an arrangement should relate to the style and decoration of the room in which it is placed, be wary of matching flowers to decorations exactly: there can often be something very calculated about such arrangements.

Echo and offset the colours of your rooms with your flowers, simply by avoiding using colours that seem to you to look unattractive together. Sometimes it will be the colour of the wood in your room or the pattern of your curtains, carpet or wallpaper that gives you the idea for a combination of flowers. At other times it will be the mix of flowers outside in the garden. Whatever prompts you to choose certain flowers and shapes, be bold in them.

Flowers and houses

Although flowers are amazingly adaptable, the age and style of the building can substantially influence arrangements.

Contemporary houses, especially those with large plate glass windows and minimalist decorations, generally suggest simple and unfussy arrangements, maybe using only one type of flower, and possibly using just one colour as well. The containers, too, should be simple both in shape and form to create the best effect.

However, many of the houses now being built have a neo-Georgian character and these and their real Georgian forebears need more classical arrangements. That is not to say that these arrangements must be formal, but they should have some of the elegance of that period. Likewise the containers need not be actual Georgian, but neither should they be starkly modern.

As well as bearing in mind the period of the house, make sure that the proportions of the arrangement are suitable, so that it relates to the height of the ceiling and the room size. So in a well-proportioned Georgian town house, for example, you can

Relaxed elegance for a traditional setting
A silver wine cooler makes a gleaming container for this wonderful mix of Iceland poppies, roses, amaryllis, parrot tulips, guelder-roses, carnations, snapdragons, broom, cow parsley, arum lilies and smilax. The studied, informal look of the arrangement is accentuated by the cleverly positioned crooked stems and casual hanging flowers.

afford to create more extravagant flower arrangements, which in a smaller modern house would look out of place. Simple combinations of flowers look best, no matter what the setting; arrangements should always look natural and never appear to have been tortured into shape. With this in mind it follows that a simple jug arrangement can look equally at home in a contemporary or Georgian setting, but whereas one type of flower, such as yellow lilies or stems of lilac, would look best in the contemporary room, a mixture of simple country flowers and foliage would be better suited to the Georgian setting.

Grand arrangements

Large-scale arrangements are often created for special occasions where a large number of people are expected and the flower arrangements must be both tall and wide in order to be seen. They are often made to display on a pedestal.

A grand arrangement is one that stands at least 90cm (3ft) tall. Although it is possible to cut foliage this long, the stems of flowers are frequently shorter. To overcome the problem, short-stemmed material is placed in funnel-like tubes, filled with water. The tubes are either inserted in the foam or wire base in the vase or, for even greater height, attached to lengths of cane, which are then fixed in the foam.

Most large arrangements are fan shaped, although this depends entirely on how many sides of the arrangement will be viewed. If, as is often the case, the arrangement is to be set against a wall, it will need to be flat backed. If, however, the arrangement is to be placed near the pulpit or the main doors of a church, it may well need to be an all-round arrangement.

For a large space in a large building, where the flowers will be seen from afar, the plant material used in an arrangement should be bold: strong-shaped leaves and vibrant-coloured flowers are essential if your creation is to make an impact.

Church pedestal arrangement
This majestic arrangement includes flowers which will stand out in the dark interior. It is composed of sweet chestnut and berberis foliage with fennel, Michaelmas daisies, 'Golden Times' roses, montbretia, larkspur and 'Uchida' lilies.

Making the arrangement (below)
First cover a wastepaper basket with hay (see p. 181), then pack in wet foam. Insert three funnels into the foam. Arrange the long-stemmed foliage in the foam in a fan shape. Add the taller flowers. Finally, pack shorter flowers and foliage in the funnels for height.

Colour

From day to day we do not take a great deal of notice of the colours that surround us: the trees and hedgerows, the walls in the rooms in which we live, or the fruit and vegetables at the greengrocers. We notice colour only occasionally, perhaps when we come to decorate or furnish a room, or when we dress for a special event. We should become more conscious of colour, and what better tutor than flowers? They grow in an extraordinary array of colours.

Do not be frightened by colour, sticking only to "safe" but boring combinations. Instead, why not experiment with using different colours? Then gradually you will come to know instinctively which colours work best together. At worst, you will create a haphazard medley of flowers or a

Vibrant colour contrast
Rich, strongly contrasting colours work together here in a lively flower combination that would look good against almost any background. The striking yellow of the tansies heightens the pinks, reds and lilacs of Peruvian lilies, statice, viburnum and melaleuca.

closely matched understatement, and both of these can look beautiful in the right setting. At best, and most often, you will create an arrangement with an inexplicable but joyful touch of magic, for flowers have a way of making this happen.

Colour theory

There are are no hard and fast rules that govern the use of colour in arrangements, although the seasonal rules offer some guidance – try using a bright mix of colours in summer, warm mellow hues in autumn, harder lines of browns and dark greens for winter and clear white, yellows and blues in spring.

Alternatively, take your cue from the colour spectrum. There are three primary colours in the colour spectrum – red, yellow and blue – and different combinations of these make the secondary colours – orange, green and purple. Varying shades and tones of all these colours are created by mixing them with white or black.

Adding drama to an arrangement (left)
*The delphiniums bring just the right amount of blue
to this large-scale, all-round, floor-standing
arrangement in a handsome terracotta pot. The other
flowers are white roses, statice and chrysanthemums
'Tokyo' and 'Tuneful'; the foliage is feathery
bottlebrush and glossy Mexican orange blossom.*

Coordinating flowers and container (above)
*This spring arrangement is informally displayed in an
old Spanish bowl whose colours link well with the
cream of the heath and narcissi and the blue grape
hyacinths and forget-me-nots. The arrangement is
strengthened by the pussy willow twigs while splashy
pink rhododendrons enhance the cool colours.*

The closer together colours are in the spectrum, the more likely they are to mix easily. You cannot go far wrong by mixing red and orange, or orange and yellow, yellow and green, green and blue, and blue and violet. This is all very well but close colour combinations can lack drama and there should be at least a little tingle of excitement in every flower arrangement.

Add excitement by choosing colours farther apart in the spectrum. Mixtures of yellow and violet, and orange and blue can look stunning. Such daring combinations should be exploited sometimes.

There are a few colours that look awful together. Some differing blues look uncomfortable when juxtaposed, and dull orange can be difficult to use successfully as

it often seems to remove the clarity of the colours near to it. In truth, though, most flower colours mix with ease and it is more a question of knowing *how much* of each colour to include to make the arrangement a pleasing whole and an exciting combination. Of course, the flowers should also relate to and not clash with the colour of the decor. So take the main colours of the room as your points of reference.

Matching colours to containers

The relationship between the colour of the container and the colours of the flowers placed in it is very important. They must work together, for the arrangement is composed of both flowers and container, and each is as important as the other.

Foliage shape and colour
Foliage is often even more varied in shape and form than flowers. This arrangement displays a diverse combination of stripes, curves, spikes, clusters and colours in a mix of Bells of Ireland, fan palm, angel wings, gaultheria, oats and milkweed.

Subdued, rustic containers like baskets will carry most combinations of flowers, whereas a brightly coloured ceramic vase might overpower many flowers.

Similarly shaped arrangements in the same container will have profoundly different effects because of the use of colour. Pastel flowers create a shimmering, misty look, while deep reds and pinks, for example, make a more emphatic statement.

However dramatic the container you choose to use, the most important thing is that the arrangement of flowers and foliage must appear inevitable.

The importance of foliage

Green is the odd man out in the colour spectrum as far as plant material is concerned because it is the colour of foliage. It always seems to exist happily with any of the other colours. In fact, it strengthens and vitalizes other colours, particularly those that are strong in tone, such as red, bright blue and yellow.

The greens of foliage are tremendously important in arrangements. They bring to life the colours of the flowers with which they are arranged. There are so many different shades to choose from: the golden yellow greens of elaeagnus, euonymus, privet and griselinia; the rich, bright greens of beech, oak, fern fronds, palm leaves, pittosporum, camellia and rhododendron; the silvery green leaves of rosemary, *Senecio* 'Sunshine', lavender, santolina and artemisia; and the dark, heavy greens of yew, box and holly. Leaf shapes vary enormously, from the fine needles of pine to the complicated latticework fronds of fern, and from the large-fingered leaves of fig to the feathery leaves of mountain ash. All contribute to an arrangement. Indeed,

Single-colour arrangement
The almost monotonal combination of dusty orange gladioli and autumnal oak foliage in an austere stoneware jar would best suit a modern interior.

a skilful arrangement featuring only foliage can look truly splendid.

Try to use a lot of green, especially the foliage of the flowers in the arrangement. It is better to limit the flowers than the foliage, as foliage gives a natural growing look to every arrangement. It offsets the forms and colours of the flowers that it is mixed with just as it does in the countryside or garden, where green is always the predominant colour, even during winter.

Shape

The very simplest kind of flower arrangement is the bunch. There are two sorts of "arranged" bunches: the posy in which the flowers are arranged in a circular fashion, to be seen from all sides; and the bouquet, in which the flowers are set out in a fan shape and designed to be seen only from the front.

By arranging posies and bouquets in vases you create two of the simplest forms of container arrangement. From a posy you can make an all-round arrangement suitable for an occasional table, and from a bouquet you can make a flat-backed arrangement for standing against a wall or mirror.

All-round arrangements

Whether circular or oval, low and simple or very tall and complicated, all-round arrangements look equally good from any

An all-round arrangement
This perfectly proportioned basket of flowers is an ideal centrepiece for a country dining table.

1 Fix a florist's prong to the base of a plastic container with adhesive clay. Place the container in the basket and fix wet foam on to the prong.

2 Make the basic all-round curve shape with eucalyptus, turning the arrangement as you work. The stems should appear to spring from the lower centre and rise above the handle. Add the carnations informally, keeping the curve.

3 *Following the line of the curve, add the ice-pink larkspur. Next, add the bright pink orchids, the delicately arching prairie gentians and the deep red godetias. Stand back to view the whole arrangement and add ingredients to fill out the shape. Top up with water so the flowers last as long as possible.*

angle. They are particularly suitable for free-standing tables such as dining tables or coffee tables, or for any location where the vase is not positioned close to a wall. Many people prefer this type of arrangement – it is lovely to be able to see through to the flowers and foliage at the back.

The best containers for all-round creations are the cylindrical and round-topped ones. Square and wide, elliptic and rectangular containers can also be suitable, and can vary from very low to quite tall vessels. Narrow vases are not so well suited to this type of arrangement and are much more effective when used for one-sided, or facing, arrangements. However, most baskets, jugs and mugs are appropriate, as are most materials.

The correct height of an all-round arrangement depends on its situation. For instance, a low arrangement is best in the centre of a dining table, so that it does not block the view of guests across the table. However, for a wide side table or to divide a room, a much taller all-round arrangement will be most attractive.

Facing arrangements

Flower arrangements that are placed against a wall where the back of the arrangement cannot be seen are known as facing, or flat-backed, arrangements. For them to work successfully, it should appear as though they are really all-round arrangements when seen from either the front or the sides. It is never attractive for these flat-backed arrangements to be placed *directly* against the wall, unless it is absolutely necessary because of restricted space, as they can easily lose their three-dimensional feel if they are too narrow. One-sided arrangements probably look at their best when they are placed against a wall or in front of a mirror.

Flat-backed arrangements do, of course, save on the number of flowers needed, as you are only looking at the display from one side. The flowers at the sides of the altar can be displayed in this way, thus saving on material. So, too, can a flower arrangement for a mantelpiece, a hall table, or a floor-standing arrangement for the corner of a room. However, the smaller the arrangement becomes, or the closer to the ground it is to stand, the more unlikely it is that you will be able to use such an arrangement, as the back will be visible.

To arrange a flat-backed flower display, it is easiest to start with foliage first. Place this at the back of the arrangement, in a rough fan shape, level with the back of the vase. Then fill in with more foliage towards the front, before finally adding the flowers that you have decided to use.

Dining-table arrangement
This would make an unusual centrepiece for a large dining table. The base is a large plate covered with wet foam topped with moss. Stems of narcissi, tulips, ranunculus and ivy are then pushed through the moss into the foam.

A facing arrangement

Flat-backed flower arrangements suit positions where the back is not visible. This arrangement is attractively displayed on a shelf at eye level.

1 *Fill the container with wet foam. Then arrange camellia leaves and emerald feather in a fan shape at the back of the container. Use the remainder of the foliage to fill in at the front.*

2 *Cut the miniature orchid stems into two sections and place with the cream freesias in the wet foam, following the shape of the foliage.*

3 *Add the roses, broom and Peruvian lilies. The stems of Peruvian lilies can be split into five or six pieces, and as these are the most delicate it is best to insert them last.*

Fragrance

Every bit as important as colour and shape, the perfume of flowers varies from sweet and delicate to strong and spicy. Take every chance to use scented flowers in your arrangements and in any gifts of bouquets and posies you offer. A room perfumed with flowers is wonderful, and there is nothing nicer than to receive a present of flowers that not only look beautiful but impart their delicious and highly individual scents to a room.

Spring and summer scents

Spring arrangements can be full of scent. There are the delicious hyacinths and many of the varieties of narcissus, especially jonquils and the very popular 'Trevithian'. But when thinking of scented flowers, roses are the first that come to mind.

Although roses with little or no scent can be used in arrangements for their unusual colours or shapes, try to incorporate at least a few roses with that delicious sweet, fruity "tea" scent in your summer arrangements: that scent is what summer is all about. The earliest flowering roses, such as the simple varieties like 'Canary Bird', tend to have little or no scent. Fortunately, however, the powerfully scented lily-of-the-valley also flowers at this time. As well as looking beautiful in an arrangement, they more than make up for the lack of scent in the roses.

Accent on scent
Two perfumes emanate from this simple arrangement. The sweet scent of the hyacinths carries beautifully in the air, whereas you need to draw close to the violets to smell their delicate perfume.

Perfumes of springtime
There are a host of spring flowers with delicious scents that can be used in arrangements to perfume your rooms. Here (from left to right) are: buttery-scented grape hyacinths and sweet polyanthus; spicy hyacinths and wattle; violets; aromatic wax flowers and sweet lily-of-the-valley; and, finally, peppery tulips with sprays of heady lilac. Other spring flowers with sweet perfumes include narcissus and mimosa.

If you are lucky enough to live in an area where the climate is mild, you can grow *Rosa banksiae* – so profuse in Italy and the south of France – with its fragrance of rich violets. Its little creamy-yellow flowers are a delight to look at and its scent, sheer joy. Some of the best scents, however, belong to the old roses: the heady-scented Damasks and Hybrid Musks, the clear, sweet-scented Rugosas and, from among the China roses, those with a rich tea scent. More and more roses are now being produced that have both the beautiful looks of the old-fashioned roses, with their flat, well-quartered flowers, and delicious scents. This makes a welcome change after several decades of roses produced only for their Hybrid Tea shapes, which often had little or no scent.

Few people are aware that at this time of year, irises have a very special perfume. The scent has a strange quality about it, often very sweet and violet-like with a slight rubbery smell on top. It sounds horrible but it isn't at all. Then there are the sweet peas. Their flower petals resemble butterflies and, like butterflies, their perfume wafts lightly and delicately on the air, one small bunch easily scenting a room.

With the arrival of high summer come the pinks, with their clove scents, and the lilies. Strongest scented of all the lilies are the auratum lilies, whose scent is very nearly overpowering: richly spicy, like concentrated nutmeg and vanilla. The perfume of the tobacco plant is similar, although not quite so heavy. Surprisingly, its flowers last quite well after picking and are ideal for arrangements.

Autumn and winter scents
Autumn flowers tend to be better known for their vibrant colours and abundant blooms than their fragrance. None the less, in autumn, the belladonna lily with its pink or white blooms is in flower, giving out a sugary, medicinal scent. Also at this time,

the long-lasting *Lilium speciosum rubrum*, with its toffee-scented blooms, adds fragrance to a floral display.

In winter no garden is complete without winter-sweet – *Chimonanthus praecox*. This is a deciduous wall shrub that looks quite ordinary for most of the year, but in mid-winter produces a crop of beautiful creamy, wax-like bells with a really strong fragrance, reminiscent of gardenias. Unfortunately, it takes a few years to

flower, but it is well worth a place in the garden, as a few flowering twigs brought inside will perfume a room for several days. Winter heliotrope is another winter-flowerer; it produces stems of delicate pink flowers with a honey-like scent, which are surrounded by unusual, almost circular, leaves.

In late winter, witch hazel – *Hamamelis mollis* – grows strange, spidery, yellow flower petals with the most delicious scent.

Perfumes of summertime
Summer is the sweetest time of year for scent. The most fragrant summer flowers of all are the sweet peas and roses, but paeonies, irises and pinks also have lovely perfumes. Why not take the opportunity to give a friend or relative a posy or bouquet of scented flowers to fill their home with summer fragrance?

Tea roses (below)
This simple bunch has a gloriously fruity scent.

Lilies (right)
Their opulent fragrance is especially strong in the evenings.

Sweet peas (right)
These delicate blooms have a unique sweetness.

Tuberoses and honeysuckle (below)
*Combined with lemon-scented
geranium leaves, they make a
heady perfume.*

Lavender and rosemary (right)
*The authentic scent of a
traditional cottage garden.*

Stocks and phlox (left)
*Two highly scented flowers for an
intensely spicy
bouquet.*

Freesias (right)
*The coloured
single flowers
have the best
perfume.*

Choosing containers

Every flower arrangement that we create in a container is like a three-dimensional painting set on the wall of a room, and it is the *whole* effect of the flowers and container, and their relationship to the surroundings that is important. Flower arrangements have an advantage over still-life paintings, though: they do not last for ever so there is no chance of becoming bored with them.

The combination of flowers and container is crucial to the success of the arrangement. Sometimes flowers will cry out for a particular container and sometimes a container will immediately suggest a selection of flowers to be arranged in it. So a coffee cup decorated with roses, for example, seems perfect filled with matching old-fashioned roses. Equally, lavender and clary will look especially attractive in a basket made from

Wicker-basket container
The wheat complements the texture of this basket while contrasting strongly with the successful combination of bright anemones and rich hydrangeas.

lavender stems. Sometimes it will be the colours and texture of a container that suggest which flowers to use in the arrangement. Of course, it is not always possible to fill a container with exactly the flowers it demands, but it is good to try.

Arrangements always work best when the container and the flowers seem absolutely meant for each other; where colours and forms complement each other, from the shape and decorations of the vase to the flowers and leaves themselves. Certainly, there are many containers that are unexacting.

Ceramic containers

The range of ceramics you can use is enormous. In general, plain-coloured vases or those with abstract or geometric designs, rather than those that are over-decorated with flowers, are the most satisfactory in which to create arrangements. If you have an attractively shaped vase with an ugly pattern or design, remember that you can cover it with some cloth or plant material.

Many combinations of flowers will look good in ceramic vases in shades of white. However, shape is important here. Allow the form of the vase to dictate the shape of the arrangement. A bulbous goldfish bowl of a vase invariably requires a generously curved creation, whereas a tall, straight-sided vase demands tall, straight spires of flowers. This is not to say that it would be impossible to do the reverse, but it is safer to follow this guide.

Using baskets

Basket shapes vary from the traditional, deep, flower-gathering trug to square ones designed for shopping. All can be lined and used for floral arrangements.

Baskets always look attractive filled with flowers, especially the more rustic, twiggy ones, which are made all over the world. All sorts of plant material are used to make these baskets, from the traditional willow

Vase dictates form
The stems of the blue African lily continue the curve of *this art nouveau vase and twisting spires of loosestrife* *and sprigs of solanum echo the theme.*

Glass sugar-bowl
The brilliant blue of these gentians needs no *enhancement so the simple, understated glass bowl makes an ideal container for this breakfast tray.*

Earthenware (right)
These huge, proud sunflowers still seem to spring straight from the soil when viewed in this roughly shaped, semi-glazed example of peasant pottery.

Cup and saucer (below)
A fine china Belleek cup and saucer make the perfect container for an exciting arrangement of spurge, everlasting pea, lavender, wild pansy, cotton lavender, tricyrtis, dead nettle and mint. The green of the spurge echoes the shamrock on the white glaze.

to scented thyme and lavender branches, and from olive and bamboo to palm and vines. A basket *is* plant material, and that is why plant material looks so appropriate.

Household items

You need not confine your floral arrangements to conventional vases or baskets. Keep a constant look-out for simple household receptacles, such as cups, mugs, jugs, wastepaper baskets and casseroles, all of which can be used to good effect. Eighteenth- and nineteenth-century pieces of china make lovely containers and can be inexpensive, especially if they are cracked. They can always be lined if they leak and if the vase is beautiful, the cracks will add authenticity.

Similarly, it is not always easy to find metal and stone containers, though you may have a wine cooler, attractive biscuit or tea tin or stone mortar tucked away in the kitchen that can be brought into service as a flower container. Copper bowls and brass cachepots also make good containers.

Glass vases

Glass is a wonderful medium for flowers. Clear glass containers, so long as the stems of your flowers are in good condition, can show off your arrangement very effectively. Depending on the shape of the vase, the stems become magnified.

Glass containers range in shape from enormous goldfish bowls to elegant single-specimen and delicate, opaque vases.

Terracotta, earthenware and wood

Warm earthenware and terracotta pots also make decorative containers. Because terracotta is porous, however, it will be necessary to line the container with plastic. Wooden containers also need to be lined in this way. Their rustic quality serves as a suitable companion to simple country flowers, making them just right for informal cottage-garden arrangements.

· CHAPTER THREE ·

FRESH
FLOWERS FOR
SPECIAL
OCCASIONS

Hardly a week of the year goes by
without some sort of special occasion.
It may be a friend's birthday, a wedding
anniversary, or a small lunch party. Then
there are all the high days and holidays
such as Christmas, Easter, and
Thanksgiving and, of course, weddings.
Flowers play an important part in all
these festivities; they have been used
as symbols of celebration through the
ages by people from every country in the
world. Whether the occasion is formal or
informal, there is nothing like flowers for
making us feel welcome.

It is a good idea to keep the flower
displays for special occasions very
seasonal. Now that it is possible to buy a
wide range of flowers throughout the
year, it is important to be selective and
to choose flowers that suit the season as
closely as possible.

Arrangements for Valentine's Day
*Red roses are the traditional Valentine's Day gift,
but the arrangements here use them in more unusual
ways. A single rose among delicate white and cream
flowers (left) is always striking, while the basket
arrangement mixes miniature roses with sprigs of fern
and frothy gypsophila sprays.*

Bouquets and posies

Flowers make an excellent present for every occasion. Every flower contains a message of transformation and growth, of joy and sunshine. Whether a pretty posy of flowers from the garden or assembled by a florist or an extravagant bouquet, a gift of flowers always gives immense pleasure. The very impermanence of flowers makes them all the more precious, a happy experience to remember.

Posies for gifts

A posy, or all-round bunch of flowers, decorated with a bow makes an ideal present for a simple occasion. You might give a posy to your host or hostess at a lunch, coffee or tea party, or to say thank you for a helping hand, or to cheer up someone. A posy is an ideal way to say, "I am thinking about you" and makes a lovely gift for a child to offer.

Children's posies
Small posies of flowers are perfect gifts for children to give. Using scented flowers is a delightful idea.

Summer tribute (above)
Poppies are magical, especially when fully open. Here they are mixed with gypsophila.

Spring present (above)
The delicacy of this mixture of pale pink broom, hyacinths and white anemones is heightened by the dramatic red bow.

Another spring gift (left)
The paperwhites and soleil d'or narcissus are deliciously sweet.

Fragrant posy
(below)
*A delightful mixed posy,
composed of scented
peach roses and cream
freesias, together with
pink cornflowers,
variegated privet and
eucalyptus.*

Arranging a posy
(above)
*It is often a simple
matter to arrange such a
posy. When laid open on
its side, the flowers
almost arrange
themselves. You could
alternatively arrange the
flowers separately,
perhaps dividing them
by colour.*

Bear in mind the language of flowers and give a posy that has special meaning. It adds a special charm and, since many of the meanings attributed to flowers are joyful, it is easy to find flowers to do the talking for you. Give a red rose to say, "I love you", daisies for "innocence", some honeysuckle for "devoted affection", some ivy for "fidelity", some tulips for "fame" and hazel catkins for "reconciliation". To make the present and the message last a little longer all the recipient need do is pop the whole posy into a jug or vase.

Bouquets for giving
Whether they contain one sort of flower or a pretty mix of flowers and foliage, bouquets are usually simple to make and always a pleasure to receive. A bouquet is the perfect gift to take to a friend who has invited you for lunch or dinner, or for a neighbour who is ill or who has done you a favour. A bouquet also makes a lovely birthday or anniversary gift, especially if the flowers chosen convey a special meaning.

Although many bouquets are easy to make, it is important not simply to bunch

1

2

1 *Begin to create this fan-shaped bouquet with three fronds of fern, the tallest in the centre. Set two single chrysanthemums on top of the middle fern so that the flower-heads sit just below the top of it. Place slightly shorter-stemmed Peruvian lilies on either side of the single chrysanthemums.*

Summer bouquet
The warm, complementary tones of the flowers – chrysanthemums, carnations, gerbera, Peruvian lilies and gypsophila – are cooled by the refreshing greens of kerria foliage and fern fronds.

together any flowers that happen to be to hand. Consider carefully your choice of flowers, making sure that the colours combine happily, and include some scented flowers to make it even more pleasurable to receive. Freesias, pinks and sweet-smelling roses can all look lovely in bouquets. If you have none to pick in your garden, you can always buy them from your local flower shop. And make a point of trying to use some unusual forms and textures when combining several sorts of flower and foliage in your bouquet.

A bouquet can be any size you choose, ranging from a small bouquet of freesias and gypsophila or one composed of pinks and some silvery foliage, to a much grander bouquet of lilies, spray carnations and chrysanthemums. Always make the character of the recipient and the nature of the occasion your guide.

Once removed from its wrapping, the bouquet can be either arranged in a single vase, or split up and transformed into several smaller arrangements to be used in various rooms around the house.

3 *Continue layering the flowers, offsetting the shapes, colours and textures as you work down the bouquet. Where the stems overlap – usually about a sixth of the way up – tie a narrow ribbon, and, to finish, attach a complementary bow (see p. 153).*

3

2 *Keeping the longest stems roughly at the centre of the bouquet, add some of the larger-flowered gerbera, the carnations and the kerria foliage. Make sure the shape is even. Place a layer of light, airy gypsophila over and around the flowers.*

Entertaining with flowers

To make good food that much more delicious, simply add flowers, not only as decoration for the table, breakfast tray, or picnic rug, but also to garnish any sort of dish, from salads and sandwiches to fish and fruit, and from cakes and confections to meat and vegetables. A single rose or a few flowers arranged in a vase can make a simple meal seem a little bit special. Likewise, the ritual Sunday morning breakfast in bed with the papers is brightened no end by the addition of a few flowers on the breakfast tray, even if you have to put them there yourself! Of course, it is even better when the flowers – and the breakfast – arrive as a waking surprise.

Whether you are planning a lunch for friends, a Sunday roast for eight, a romantic dinner for two, or a grand dinner party, make sure you include an arrangement or two to help create a relaxed atmosphere.

Arrangements for such occasions need not be elaborate. In fact, a single flower would make the perfect table centrepiece at the dinner for two. Reflect some of the colours of the room, tablecloth or napkins, even the colours of the food, in the flowers you choose, and try using some fruit or vegetables in the arrangement. Cherries, blackberries, strawberries, curly kale, cabbage leaves and sprigs of herbs can all look absolutely beautiful amongst flowers.

For a candle-lit dinner under the night sky, try scented white flowers. A summer picnic demands a crock of brilliant blooms whose colours sing out loud. The vivid reds and yellows of tropical flowers would match an exotic dinner in a conservatory.

Facing arrangement for a sideboard
This mixture of fruits, vegetables and flowers would make a sumptuous arrangement for a dinner party. Grapes, vine and fig leaves, mulberries, blackberries, nectarines, pineapple, runner beans, ornamental cabbage leaves, crab apples, pears and dahlias combine in a memorable celebration of plenty.

Nasturtium and lettuce salad
(above)
*Nasturtium flowers have a tangy
taste like watercress and their
bright colour is perfectly set off by
the pale green lettuce. Marigold,
dandelion and pink runner-bean
flowers are a non-edible decoration.
This is ideal served with a walnut-
oil dressing.*

Chicory and herb salad (left)
*A delicious mix of cool colours, this
salad has a base of chicory with the
edible flowers of fennel and young
chives added as decoration. Serve
with a lime dressing.*

Flowers with food

Many flowers are good to eat, and it is
undoubtedly true that the more beautiful a
dish looks, the more delicious it tastes.
There are plenty of edible flowers that can
be added to salads. The startling red, orange
and yellow flowers of tasty nasturtiums
make a strong visual impact when set
against the bright greens of lettuce or dark
greens of spinach, pale chicory or frilly
endive. Sweet-scented rose petals,
marigolds, violets, primroses, fruit tree
blossoms and the flowers of many herbs all
make beautiful garnishes to a dish.

Mother's Day

Mother's Day is a special occasion when flowers make a lovely gift. Giving a present for Mother's Day is a relatively new tradition, but of all the presents to choose from, flowers are the most popular. On this occasion, it is nice to give flowers that convey a message; as many of the meanings from the language of flowers are to do with the pleasant things of life, it is not difficult to find a combination of flowers that look beautiful together, and at the same time convey some feelings about your relationship with your mother.

You could make a bouquet of roses, meaning "love", with stocks for "lasting beauty" and gillyflowers for "bonds of affection". Or you could combine yellow lilies, meaning "gaiety", with bright red chrysanthemums for "I love" and daffodils for "regard". Other appropriate flowers are bluebells, meaning "constancy", and red tulips as a "declaration of love".

Both bouquets and arrangements of flowers make popular presents and in each case the presentation is all important. A bouquet needs to be crisply wrapped in cellophane with a bow that matches the flowers, while an arrangement should be carefully prepared with an eye on its composition, and prettily beribboned.

Flowers with a message
This pretty basket makes a perfect Mother's Day gift. The white roses are a sign of love while daisies are a symbol of patience. White irises, meaning "message", complete the delightful arrangement.

Easter

The most important festival in the Christian calendar is Easter. At this time of year the churches are decorated with arrangements of lilies, with their great white trumpets and soft, sweet scent. To decorate your home, and for a festive change, make a flowery Easter nest using the seasonal flowers available in your garden and some hand-painted eggs, the traditional symbol of rebirth and renewal.

Making an Easter nest

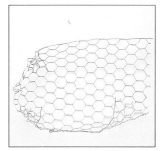

1 *Cut a rectangle from a piece of chicken-wire using wire cutters. Then fold and tuck in the corners to form a nest shape.*

2 *Thread a stub wire needle with raffia and sew clumps of hay and alder twigs on to the wire frame to make the nest.*

3 *Line the nest with a water-holding container and fill with wet foam. Arrange the flowers and eggs in the foam.*

Easter celebration
The completed nest displays a mixture of glowing yellow, pink and fresh green flowers and foliage surrounding a cluster of hand-painted eggs that echo those colours. Any combination of simple flowers can be used to achieve the informal look. This arrangement uses Cape cowslips, flowering-currant twigs, the single chrysanthemum 'Tuneful', the polyanthus 'Pacific Hybrid' and tiny orchids.

Weddings

The wedding ceremony is one of the most important ceremonies of our lives and because of this the event can be rather overwhelming. However, amid all the formality of the occasion, flowers can provide a welcome element. So it is well worth making that extra effort to create beautiful arrangements.

The bride usually carries a bouquet of flowers, and this can take a variety of forms, ranging from a simple bunch of garden flowers to a much more elaborate bouquet where the flowers are wired so that they can overflow in a delicate shower of blooms and foliage. The style and colours of the flowers used depend on the type of wedding and the design of the bride's dress. A bunch of lilies can make an elegant bouquet to be carried in the crook of the bride's arm, or, for a more informal wedding, a simple posy can be just right.

Then there are the flowers for the bride's hair. Again, they can be simple, single flowers or a circlet or half-circlet of flowers that garland her head.

Bridesmaids, too, usually carry flowers. They can be similar to those the bride carries, although it is more usual for bridesmaids to carry small posies rather than a shower bouquet. If they are small children, they can carry little baskets or small hoops of flowers, or maybe even a pretty ball of flowers hanging from a ribbon. The bridesmaids' flowers should complement the colour and style of their dresses, and relate to the bride's flowers.

Buttonholes
(right and below)
Traditional and more unusual decorations for groom and guests:
1 *orchid – a favourite flower for weddings – with camellia leaves;*
2 *peach rose with eucalyptus leaves;*
3 *a simple white rose. (See pp. 189–90 for wiring flower stems.)*

Flowery comb for a bridesmaid (above and top)
Assemble three small bunches of your chosen flowers and foliage (see pp. 189–90 for wiring). Cover the stub wire with tape and then wire one bunch of flowers to the comb, covering the tie with tape. Wire on the other two bunches to overlap the first. Leave 2cm (1in) of wire at each end in order to secure the decoration to the comb by twisting the ends between the teeth.

Making the bride's bouquet

1 *Wire all the ingredients individually to strengthen and lengthen stems (see pp. 189–90).*

2 *Begin making the trail by binding some ferns, flowers and foliage together with reel wire.*

3 *Wire in more flowers one by one to establish the triangular shape of the trail.*

4 *Cover the wire with tape as you go. Complete the trail by bending the stems below the flowers.*

5 *Add the remaining material above the trail, binding the wires near the bend. Spread the flowers.*

6 *Leaving ends to trail, bind ribbon down and up the handle. Tie the ends and add a bow (see p. 153).*

Trailing bouquet for a bride
Although this bouquet is time-consuming to make, the end result looks sumptuous with its sparkling white flowers and silver and green foliage; it also has a delightful, fresh perfume. The flowers and foliage used are lilies-of-the-valley, heather sprigs, orchids, stephanotis flowers, rosemary sprigs, ivy, larkspur, senecio, white roses and fern fronds.

Preparing wedding flowers

All the flowers that are carried or worn at a wedding have to be prepared only a short while before the ceremony as they will soon begin to wilt. Before arranging them, it is best to give them a good, long drink of water. Carnations and spray carnations, single chrysanthemums, freesias, Peruvian lilies, stephanotis, gypsophila and half-open roses all last quite well and can be prepared up to 12 hours in advance, so long as they are then kept in a cool place. It is not a good idea to keep them in the refrigerator, however, as this is *too* cold and the flowers can easily become frosted. Sweet peas, full blown roses, Christmas roses and lilies-of-the-valley are more short-lived.

Flowers for the church

Just as important as the flowers for the bride, bridesmaids and guests are the flowers that decorate the church. It looks lovely if these can echo the colours of the bride's flowers, but bear in mind that churches are brightly lit. Often very pale or very bright flower arrangements look best.

There are usually two substantial flower arrangements made for inside the church, one on either side of the altar, that can be seen from every position. It is also a nice idea to have an arrangement near the entrance to welcome everyone. Window ledges can also be decorated, pillars can be garlanded and arrangements can also be made for the pew ends.

Flower sphere (below)
This pretty ball on long, pink ribbons is a charming mixture of tiny cream and pink roses, smilax and laurustinus. To prepare the base, soak a foam sphere (see below left) in water. Double over a piece of heavy gauge stub wire and push it through the sphere, leaving a wire loop sticking out of the foam. Bend the two ends back and secure to the loop. Thread a ribbon through the loop, tie the ends together and hang the ball up. Stud the foam with flowers and foliage to cover and finally attach a bow to the ribbon.

Flower basket
(above)
A basket of delicate little flowers look very pretty and is easy for a young bridesmaid to carry. The colours of the flowers should complement the colour of her dress. This arrangement uses miniature cream and pink roses, statice, leather fern and heather.

Base for flower sphere

Pew end for special guests

Pew ends provide a glowing welcome. These flowers will last well because they are fixed in wet foam. The arrangement is comprised of decorative cabbage, speciosum lily, montbretia, Michaelmas daisies, fennel, berberis, larkspur, yellow roses and beech foliage. Bouquets could also be hung, but they would have to be made at the last minute to ensure that they look fresh throughout the ceremony.

Making a pew end

1 *Fill the hanging frame with foam, dampened and trimmed to fit. Then fix the cabbage into the central compartment on top of the frame.*

2 *Insert the shorter flowers around the cabbage, filling in at the back. Add the taller lily, montbretia and foliage to form the trail.*

Harvest time and Thanksgiving

With autumn comes the ripening of many crops: cereals, apples, pears, pomegranates, persimmons and melons, nuts and grapes, artichokes and sweet corn, pumpkins and multicoloured peppers. Churches are laden with the fruits of the harvest: even those in the cities manage to have wondrous displays of gold and rust and yellow. These colours are echoed by the many varieties of chrysanthemum and dahlia, strawflower and gladioli that flower in profusion at this wonderful time of year.

The celebration of the harvest is one of the most ancient of all festivals, dating from pagan times when communities were dependent on the success of their own crops. Today, we are not nearly so aware of the quality of the harvest. Even after a very wet and sunless summer, when the farmers have been complaining that the harvest will be poor, there are still bountiful supplies of harvest fruits and vegetables in the shops.

Harvest thanksgiving is a time to celebrate at home and to reflect on the effects of the seasons on our lives. What better way to do this than to give a thanksgiving party with harvest decorations. Arrangements look splendid in glowing autumn colours: rich amber, sunny gold and nutty brown. Make the fruits, vegetables and cereals an integral part of your harvest arrangement, perhaps created for a thanksgiving table display, or incorporate them in some rich garlanding to be placed around a doorway or buffet table.

Autumnal celebration
A small, hollowed-out pumpkin lined with plastic forms the container for this arrangement. The late sunshine colours make this a happy combination of spindle, snowberries, Chinese lanterns, and strawflowers.

Seasonal garland

Garlands are a lovely way of decorating a door, fireplace, table, niche or painting. If you wish to make a long garland, join together individual moss-filled, chicken-wire tubes with mossing wire, and cover with more wired plant material. This one is decorated with 'Destiny' lilies, rose hips, Worcester apples, red and yellow peppers, chilli peppers, box foliage, barley, old man's beard and eucalyptus.

Making a robust garland

1 *Decide how long your garland is to be and make the appropriate number of chicken-wire tubes (see p. 183). Join them with mossing wire. Then wire the peppers, apples (see p. 171) and lilies (see p. 190).*

2 *Taking one section of tube at a time, poke the stems and wires of the ingredients into the moss. The flowers must lie in the direction in which the garland will hang. Overlap the material to hide the base.*

Christmas

The countdown to Christmas Day begins the month before with the four weeks of Advent. In many countries this period is celebrated with a wreath containing four candles, one being lit on each Sunday of the month. You can make an Advent wreath with fresh flowers and foliage and renew it each week. Even at the beginning of Advent the decorations are in evidence for Christmas. More entertaining is done at this season than at any other time of year and there are many opportunities for wonderful arrangements.

There has been a mid-winter festival since early pagan times, when boughs of evergreen, including mistletoe, conifer, holly and ivy, were brought into the house. In the fourth century, Christmas – the word is derived from Christ's Mass – was first celebrated by the Church and gradually the pagan and Christian festivals became merged. The exchanging of presents was a pre-Christian tradition; so too was the custom of having lanterns in the house, which today take the form of Christmas tree lights. The Christmas tree is quite a recent addition to the celebrations, made popular by Prince Albert, who imported large numbers of them from his estate in Coburg in 1845. Flowers and evergreen foliage now play a large part in our Christmas festivities. Christmas trees are sold in their millions and it is exciting to decorate the house with some beautiful flower arrangements and garlanding. Flower shops can supply a wide range of colourful and long-lasting flowers, as well as the familiar holly, mistletoe, ivy and pine tree branches.

The more traditional Christmas arrangements and decorations are always appreciated: a Christmas tree simply decorated a few days before Christmas with candles and bows; a wreath of holly and pine for the front door; some rich garlanding; and some arrangements in glowing colours, perhaps with candles, to brighten the hallway, living room, sideboard or the dinner table. They are part of the magic of Christmas.

Traditional circular wreath
Variegated holly and blue spruce are attached to a frame (see p. 183) and decorated with red balls and bow.

Spray wreath
Three branches of blue spruce are hung with cones, baubles and raffia strands and twists.

Christmas-party centrepiece
A useful white ceramic Lazy Susan creates the structure for this cascading arrangement. Brilliant red and green keynotes are established with red roses and vigorous butcher's-broom foliage. Rowan clusters, snowberries and green candles develop the theme.

Christmas garlands

Of the three different types of garlanding shown here, the robust garland would look best against a wall, maybe surrounding a mirror or window. The delicate garland would be ideal for a shelf, mantelpiece or around a painting, and the traditional swag would look good adorning a large fireplace in a living room.

Traditional garland

1 *Arrange fir branches bearing cones, overlapping them to make the shape you want to create. Tie the branches together in several places, making sure that they are held together very securely.*

2 *Fill out the garland by tying in pieces of berried holly and elaeagnus along the whole length.*

Delicate garland

Plait strands of raffia to the length you require (see p. 185). Then thread groups of gold-sprayed butcher's-broom leaves and silver-sprayed larch cone twigs into the plait at regular intervals. For an even more festive look, add wired gold balls into each clump of plant material.

Robust garland

Chicken wire stuffed with moss (see p. 183) forms the basis of this swag. Push or wire blue spruce sprigs into the frame and then thread wired fruits into the base. Add the artificial cherries last.

DRIED
FLOWERS

CHAPTER FOUR

GUIDE TO DRIED FLOWERS AND FOLIAGE

The following pages are a colour-by-colour guide to the dried flowers and plants that make the ingredients of arrangements. Some plants, such as statice (*Limonium* sp.), roses (*Rosa* sp.) and everlasting flowers (*Helichrysum* sp.), are invaluable since they grow in a profusion of different forms and colours.

The ingredients illustrated are widely available, although they originate from many regions of the world. A few of them (some cones and leaves) were gathered from the wild with great care, so as not to damage the parent plant. Always check before you pick whether the material is a protected or endangered species and never take any wild plant material that falls into this category. Ask the landowner's permission before picking anything under cultivation.

Natural riches
An array of dried flowers hanging on a wall has as much visual interest as a rich rug or tapestry. The abundant mixture of colours and textures in these bunches of roses, helipterum, strawflowers, yarrow, physalis, statice and barley complements the rustic feel of the whitewashed wall.

Reds and pinks

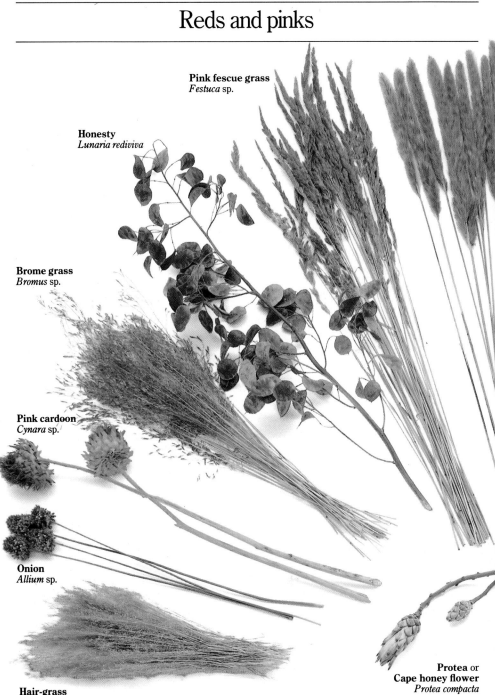

Pink fescue grass
Festuca sp.

Honesty
Lunaria rediviva

Brome grass
Bromus sp.

Pink cardoon
Cynara sp.

Onion
Allium sp.

Hair-grass
Aira sp.

Protea or
Cape honey flower
Protea compacta

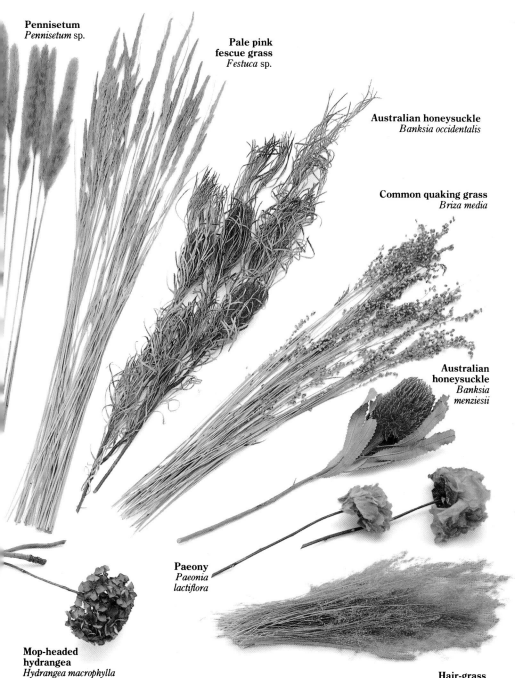

Pennisetum
Pennisetum sp.

**Pale pink
fescue grass**
Festuca sp.

Australian honeysuckle
Banksia occidentalis

Common quaking grass
Briza media

**Australian
honeysuckle**
*Banksia
menziesii*

Paeony
*Paeonia
lactiflora*

**Mop-headed
hydrangea**
Hydrangea macrophylla

Hair-grass
Aira sp.

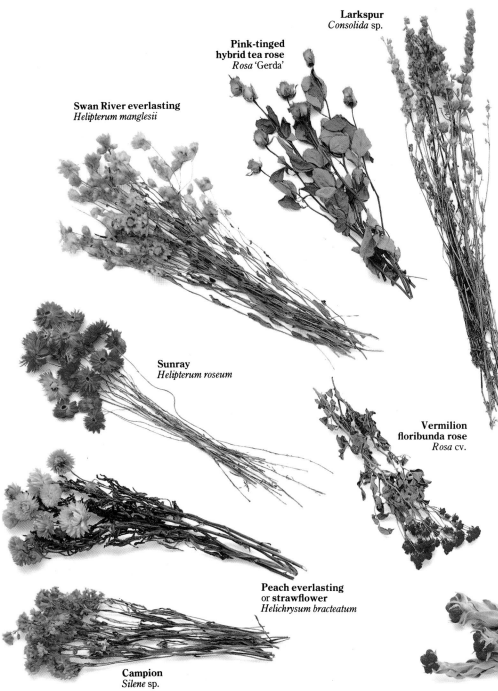

Larkspur
Consolida sp.

Pink-tinged
hybrid tea rose
Rosa 'Gerda'

Swan River everlasting
Helipterum manglesii

Sunray
Helipterum roseum

Vermilion
floribunda rose
Rosa cv.

Peach everlasting
or **strawflower**
Helichrysum bracteatum

Campion
Silene sp.

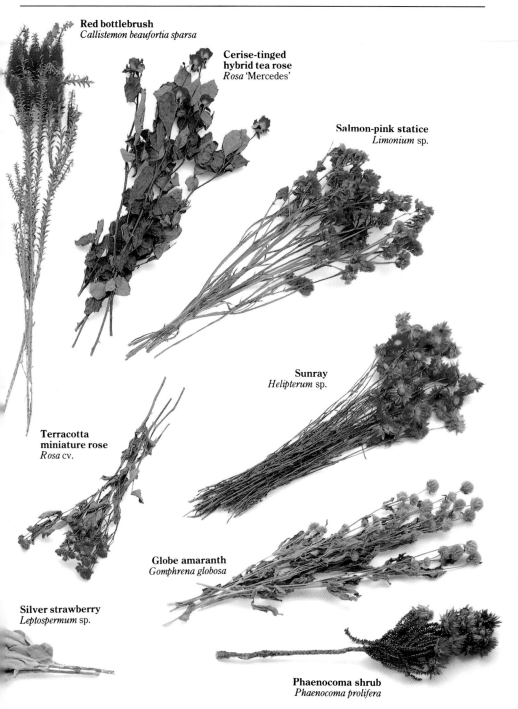

Red bottlebrush
Callistemon beaufortia sparsa

**Cerise-tinged
hybrid tea rose**
Rosa 'Mercedes'

Salmon-pink statice
Limonium sp.

Sunray
Helipterum sp.

**Terracotta
miniature rose**
Rosa cv.

Globe amaranth
Gomphrena globosa

Silver strawberry
Leptospermum sp.

Phaenocoma shrub
Phaenocoma prolifera

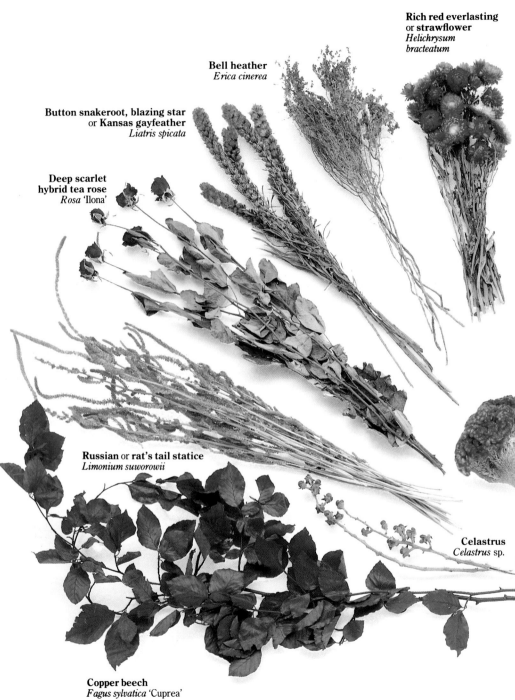

Rich red everlasting
or **strawflower**
*Helichrysum
bracteatum*

Bell heather
Erica cinerea

Button snakeroot, blazing star
or **Kansas gayfeather**
Liatris spicata

**Deep scarlet
hybrid tea rose**
Rosa 'Ilona'

Russian or **rat's tail statice**
Limonium suworowii

Celastrus
Celastrus sp.

Copper beech
Fagus sylvatica 'Cuprea'

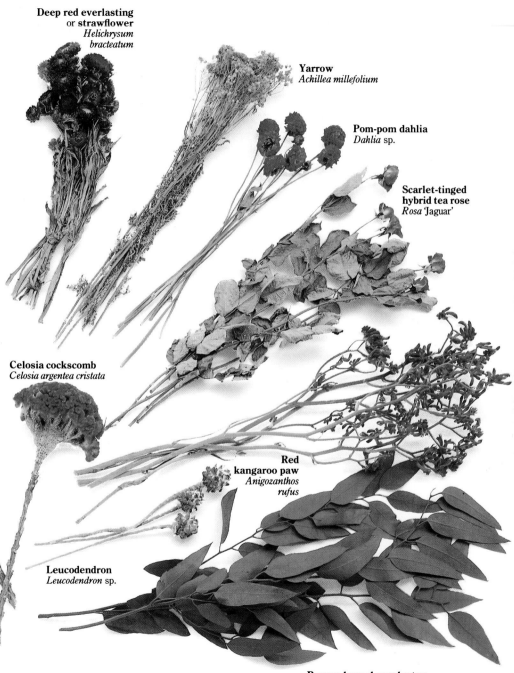

Deep red everlasting
or **strawflower**
Helichrysum
bracteatum

Yarrow
Achillea millefolium

Pom-pom dahlia
Dahlia sp.

Scarlet-tinged
hybrid tea rose
Rosa 'Jaguar'

Celosia cockscomb
Celosia argentea cristata

Red
kangaroo paw
Anigozanthos
rufus

Leucodendron
Leucodendron sp.

Bronze-leaved eucalyptus
Eucalyptus sp.

Oranges and yellows

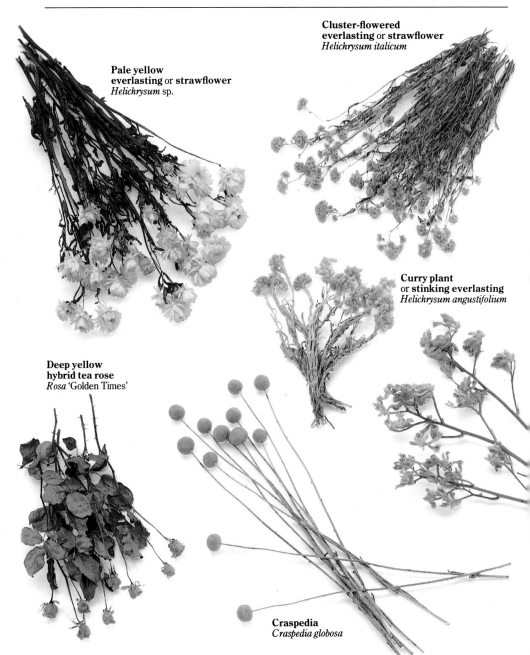

**Cluster-flowered
everlasting** or **strawflower**
Helichrysum italicum

**Pale yellow
everlasting** or **strawflower**
Helichrysum sp.

Curry plant
or **stinking everlasting**
Helichrysum angustifolium

**Deep yellow
hybrid tea rose**
Rosa 'Golden Times'

Craspedia
Craspedia globosa

Golden everlasting or **strawflower**
Helichrysum sp.

Deep yellow yarrow
Achillea filipendulina
'Coronation Gold'

Sunray
Helipterum sp.

Bronze-tinged hybrid tea rose
Rosa 'La Minuette'

Yellow kangaroo paw
Anigozanthos sp.

Silver-leaved everlasting or **strawflower**
Helichrysum sp.

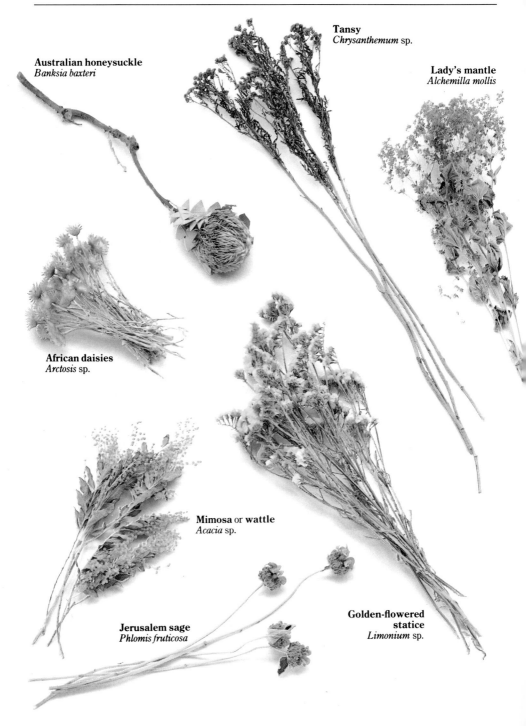

Tansy
Chrysanthemum sp.

Australian honeysuckle
Banksia baxteri

Lady's mantle
Alchemilla mollis

African daisies
Arctosis sp.

Mimosa or **wattle**
Acacia sp.

Jerusalem sage
Phlomis fruticosa

Golden-flowered statice
Limonium sp.

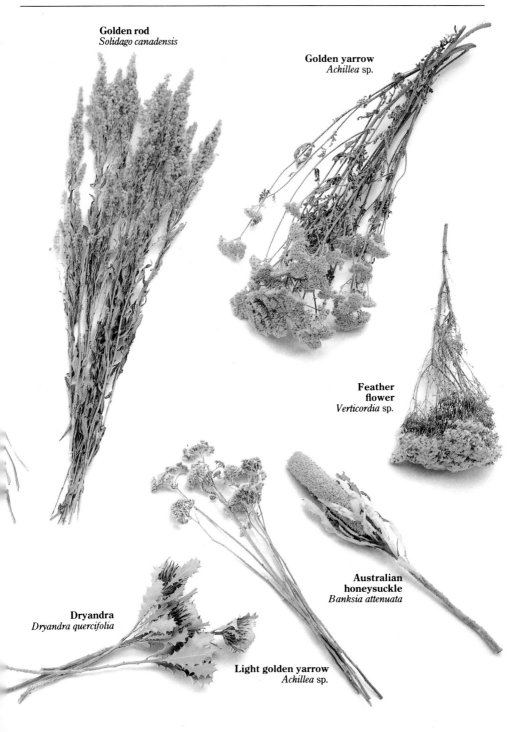

Golden rod
Solidago canadensis

Golden yarrow
Achillea sp.

**Feather
flower**
Verticordia sp.

**Australian
honeysuckle**
Banksia attenuata

Dryandra
Dryandra quercifolia

Light golden yarrow
Achillea sp.

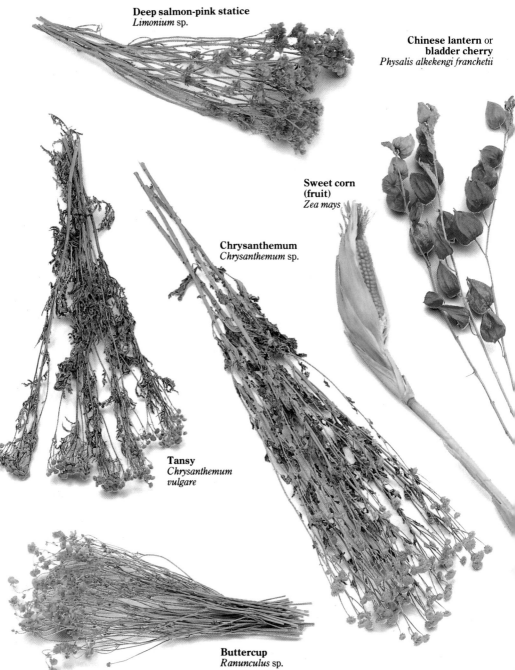

Deep salmon-pink statice
Limonium sp.

Chinese lantern or
bladder cherry
Physalis alkekengi franchetii

**Sweet corn
(fruit)**
Zea mays

Chrysanthemum
Chrysanthemum sp.

Tansy
*Chrysanthemum
vulgare*

Buttercup
Ranunculus sp.

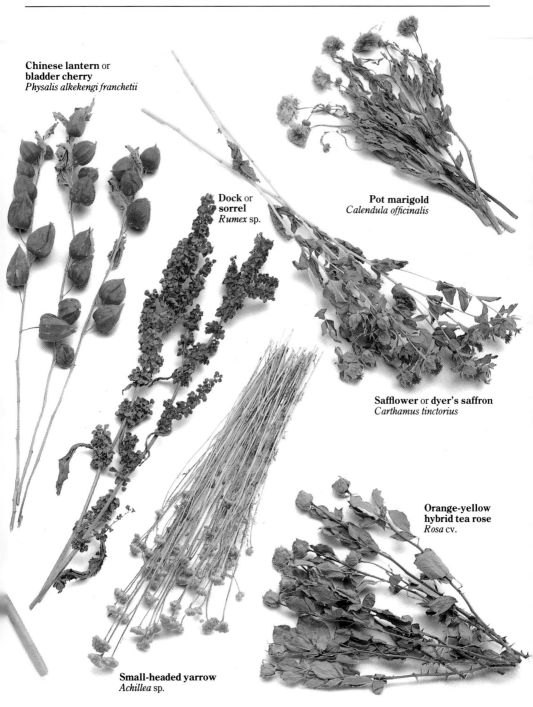

Chinese lantern or
bladder cherry
Physalis alkekengi franchetii

Dock or
sorrel
Rumex sp.

Pot marigold
Calendula officinalis

Safflower or **dyer's saffron**
Carthamus tinctorius

**Orange-yellow
hybrid tea rose**
Rosa cv.

Small-headed yarrow
Achillea sp.

Greens and browns

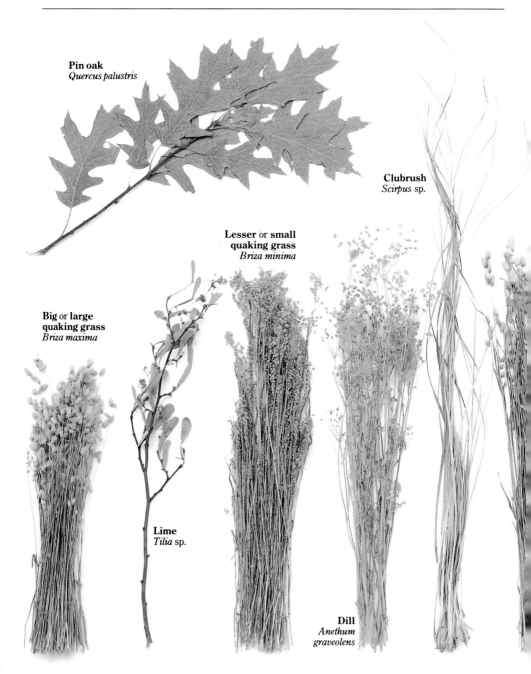

Pin oak
Quercus palustris

Clubrush
Scirpus sp.

Lesser or **small
quaking grass**
Briza minima

Big or **large
quaking grass**
Briza maxima

Lime
Tilia sp.

Dill
*Anethum
graveolens*

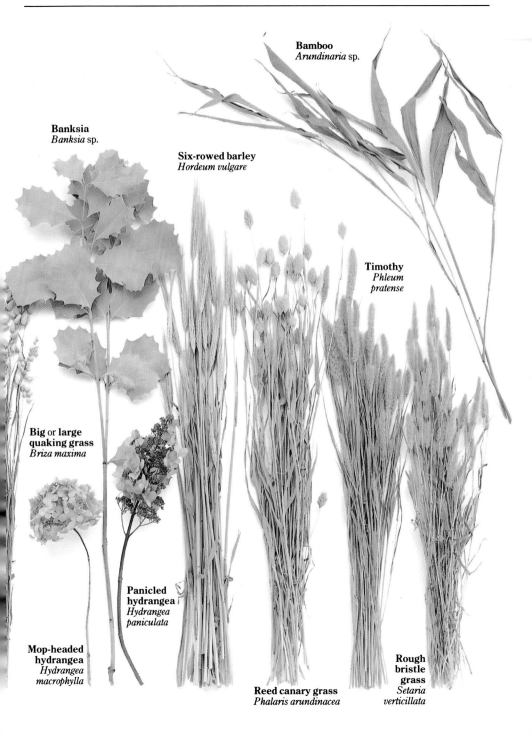

Bamboo
Arundinaria sp.

Banksia
Banksia sp.

Six-rowed barley
Hordeum vulgare

Timothy
*Phleum
pratense*

Big or **large
quaking grass**
Briza maxima

**Panicled
hydrangea**
*Hydrangea
paniculata*

**Mop-headed
hydrangea**
*Hydrangea
macrophylla*

**Rough
bristle
grass**
*Setaria
verticillata*

Reed canary grass
Phalaris arundinacea

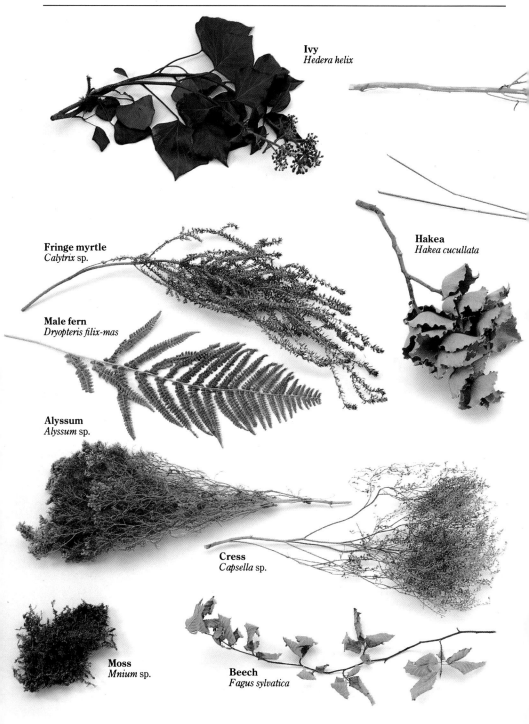

Ivy
Hedera helix

Fringe myrtle
Calytrix sp.

Hakea
Hakea cucullata

Male fern
Dryopteris filix-mas

Alyssum
Alyssum sp.

Cress
Capsella sp.

Moss
Mnium sp.

Beech
Fagus sylvatica

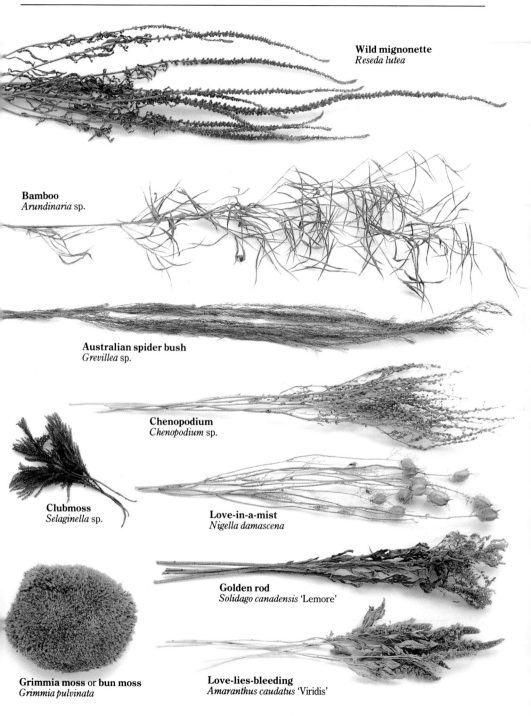

Wild mignonette
Reseda lutea

Bamboo
Arundinaria sp.

Australian spider bush
Grevillea sp.

Chenopodium
Chenopodium sp.

Clubmoss
Selaginella sp.

Love-in-a-mist
Nigella damascena

Golden rod
Solidago canadensis 'Lemore'

Grimmia moss or **bun moss**
Grimmia pulvinata

Love-lies-bleeding
Amaranthus caudatus 'Viridis'

Snow gum
Eucalyptus niphophila

Scots pine
Pinus sylvestris

Rush
Juncus sp.

Mop-headed hydrangea
Hydrangea macrophylla

Leucodendron
Leucodendron sp.

Dryandra
Dryandra sp.

Reed
Phragmites australis

Crimson bottlebrush
Callistemon citrinus

Bamboo
Arundinaria sp.

Leucodendron
Leucodendron stelligerum

Clubrush
Scirpus sp.

Mexican orange
Choisya ternata

Hakea
Hakea sp.

Reed
Phragmites australis

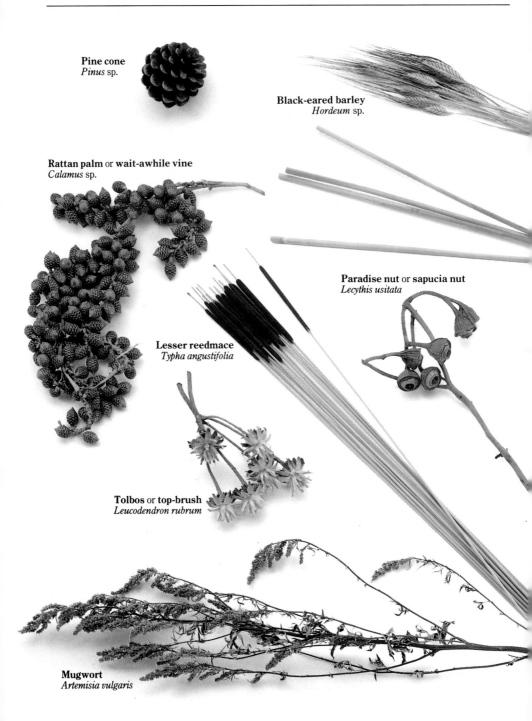

Pine cone
Pinus sp.

Black-eared barley
Hordeum sp.

Rattan palm or **wait-awhile vine**
Calamus sp.

Paradise nut or **sapucia nut**
Lecythis usitata

Lesser reedmace
Typha angustifolia

Tolbos or **top-brush**
Leucodendron rubrum

Mugwort
Artemisia vulgaris

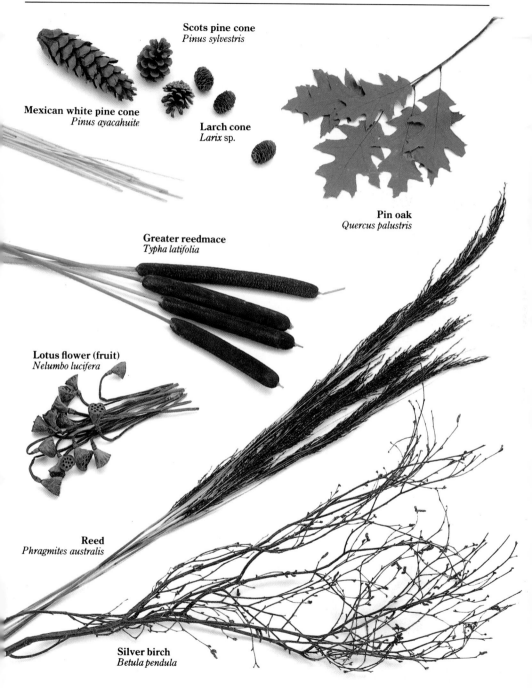

Scots pine cone
Pinus sylvestris

Mexican white pine cone
Pinus ayacahuite

Larch cone
Larix sp.

Pin oak
Quercus palustris

Greater reedmace
Typha latifolia

Lotus flower (fruit)
Nelumbo lucifera

Reed
Phragmites australis

Silver birch
Betula pendula

Millet
Milium sp.

Globe artichoke
Cynara scolymus

Love-in-a-mist
Nigella damascena

Ornamental onion
Allium aflatunense

Hop
Humulus lupulus

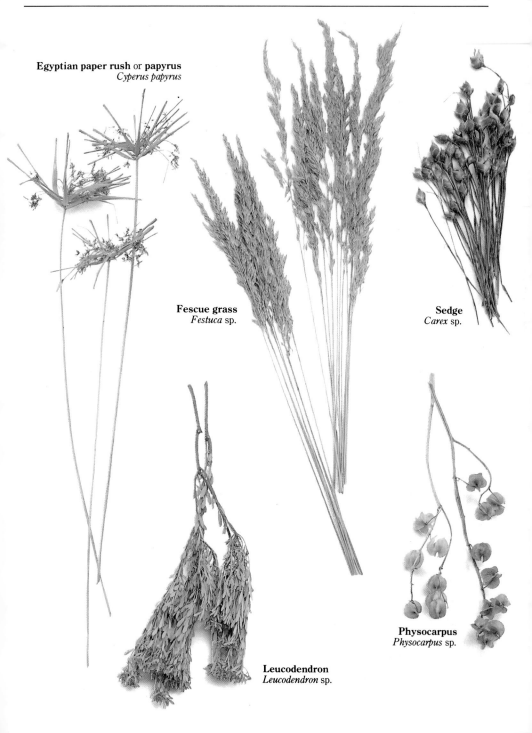

Egyptian paper rush or **papyrus**
Cyperus papyrus

Fescue grass
Festuca sp.

Sedge
Carex sp.

Leucodendron
Leucodendron sp.

Physocarpus
Physocarpus sp.

Blues and purples

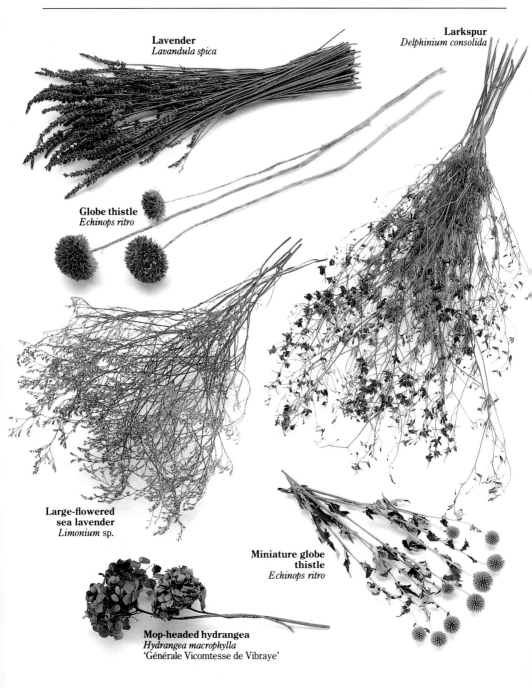

Lavender
Lavandula spica

Larkspur
Delphinium consolida

Globe thistle
Echinops ritro

**Large-flowered
sea lavender**
Limonium sp.

**Miniature globe
thistle**
Echinops ritro

Mop-headed hydrangea
Hydrangea macrophylla
'Générale Vicomtesse de Vibraye'

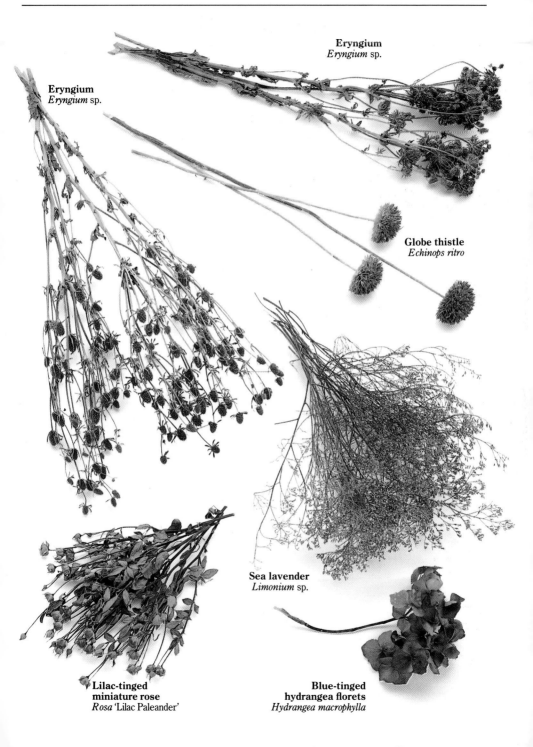

Eryngium
Eryngium sp.

Eryngium
Eryngium sp.

Globe thistle
Echinops ritro

Sea lavender
Limonium sp.

**Lilac-tinged
miniature rose**
Rosa 'Lilac Paleander'

**Blue-tinged
hydrangea florets**
Hydrangea macrophylla

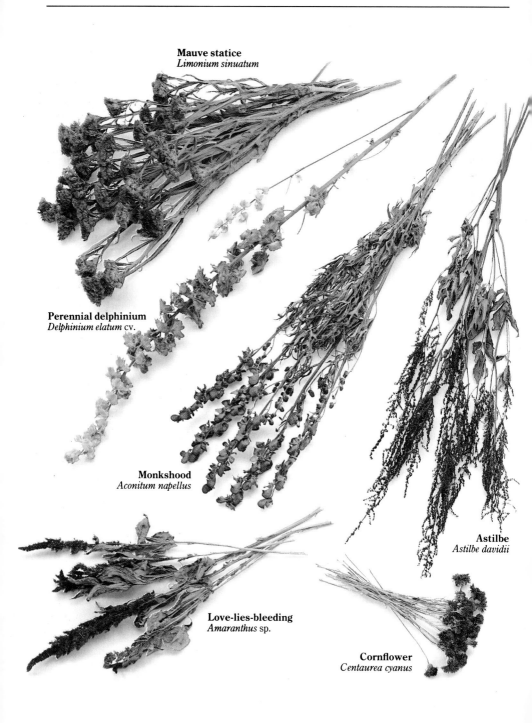

Mauve statice
Limonium sinuatum

Perennial delphinium
Delphinium elatum cv.

Monkshood
Aconitum napellus

Astilbe
Astilbe davidii

Love-lies-bleeding
Amaranthus sp.

Cornflower
Centaurea cyanus

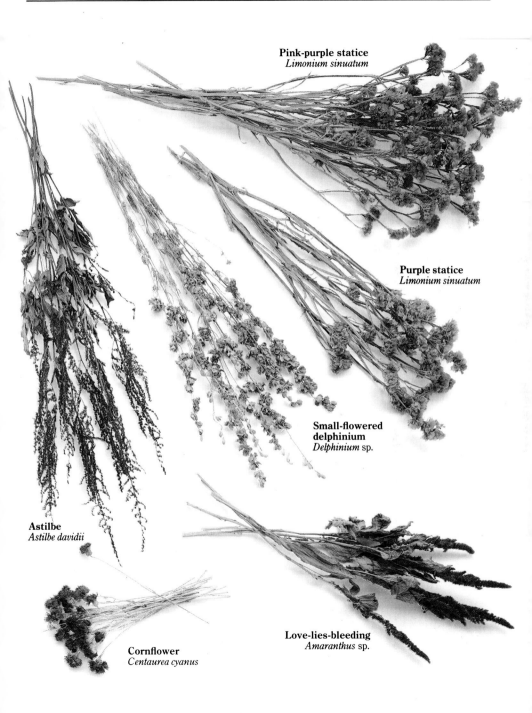

Pink-purple statice
Limonium sinuatum

Purple statice
Limonium sinuatum

Small-flowered delphinium
Delphinium sp.

Astilbe
Astilbe davidii

Cornflower
Centaurea cyanus

Love-lies-bleeding
Amaranthus sp.

Whites, creams, silvers

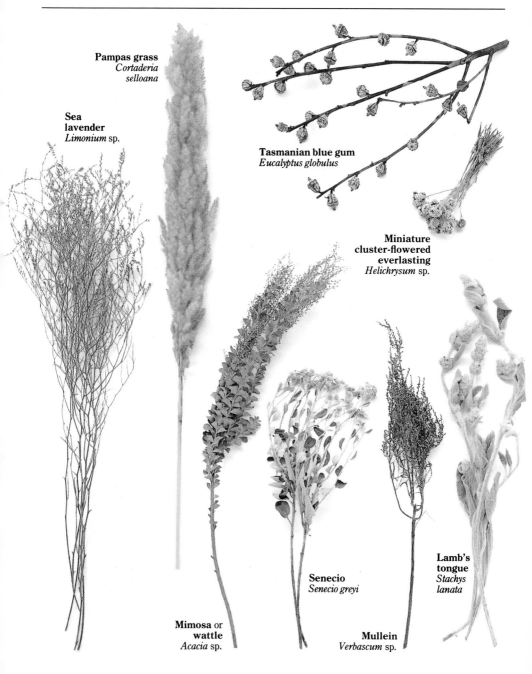

Pampas grass
*Cortaderia
selloana*

**Sea
lavender**
Limonium sp.

Tasmanian blue gum
Eucalyptus globulus

**Miniature
cluster-flowered
everlasting**
Helichrysum sp.

Senecio
Senecio greyi

**Lamb's
tongue**
*Stachys
lanata*

Mimosa or
wattle
Acacia sp.

Mullein
Verbascum sp.

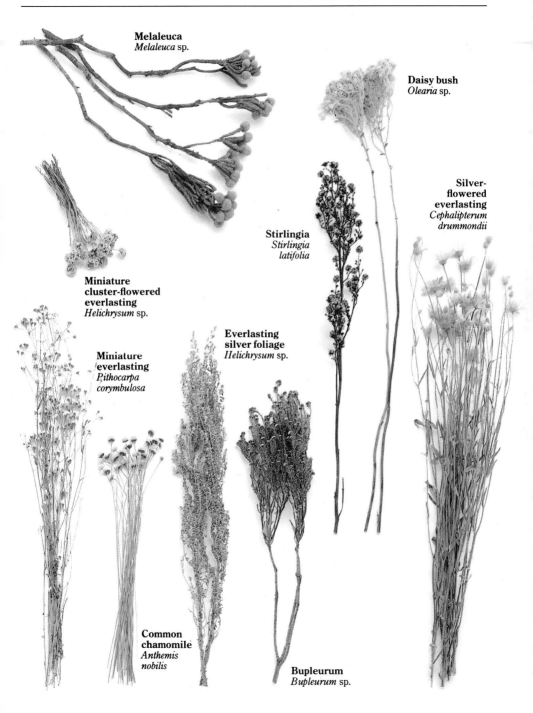

Melaleuca
Melaleuca sp.

Daisy bush
Olearia sp.

Silver-flowered everlasting
Cephalipterum drummondii

Stirlingia
Stirlingia latifolia

Miniature cluster-flowered everlasting
Helichrysum sp.

Everlasting silver foliage
Helichrysum sp.

Miniature everlasting
Pithocarpa corymbulosa

Common chamomile
Anthemis nobilis

Bupleurum
Bupleurum sp.

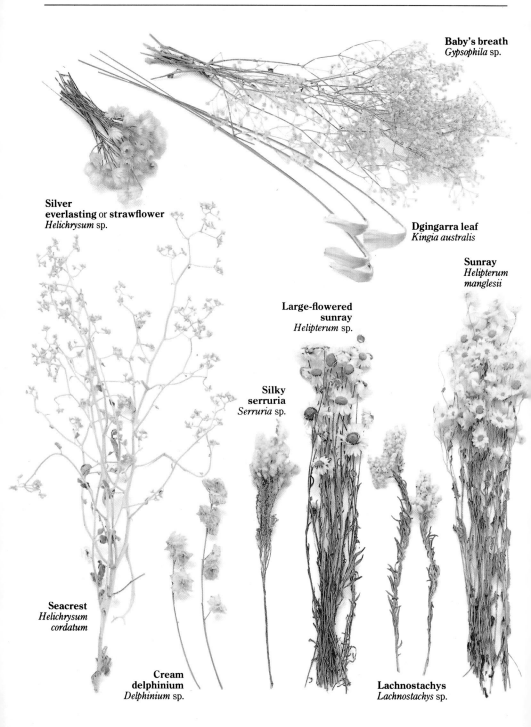

Baby's breath
Gypsophila sp.

**Silver
everlasting** or **strawflower**
Helichrysum sp.

Dgingarra leaf
Kingia australis

Sunray
*Helipterum
manglesii*

**Large-flowered
sunray**
Helipterum sp.

**Silky
serruria**
Serruria sp.

Seacrest
*Helichrysum
cordatum*

**Cream
delphinium**
Delphinium sp.

Lachnostachys
Lachnostachys sp.

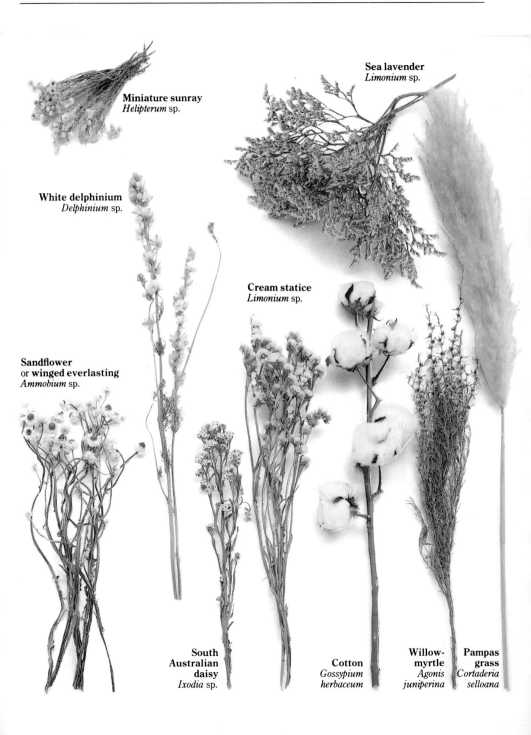

Miniature sunray
Helipterum sp.

Sea lavender
Limonium sp.

White delphinium
Delphinium sp.

Cream statice
Limonium sp.

Sandflower
or **winged everlasting**
Ammobium sp.

**South
Australian
daisy**
Ixodia sp.

Cotton
*Gossypium
herbaceum*

**Willow-
myrtle**
*Agonis
juniperina*

**Pampas
grass**
*Cortaderia
selloana*

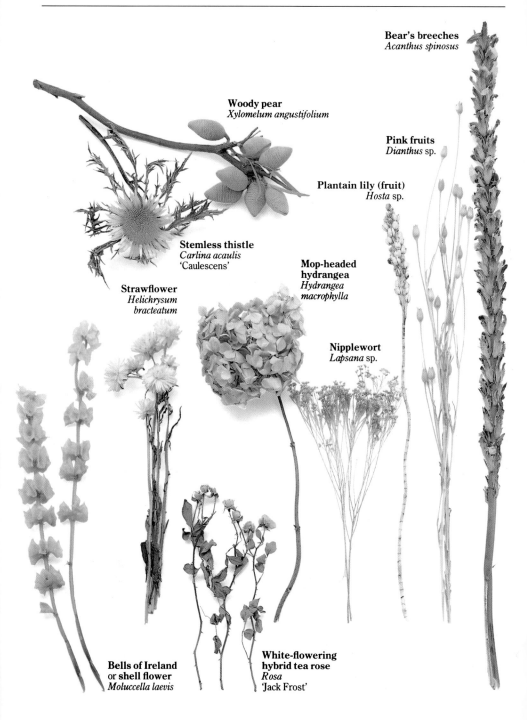

Bear's breeches
Acanthus spinosus

Woody pear
Xylomelum angustifolium

Pink fruits
Dianthus sp.

Plantain lily (fruit)
Hosta sp.

Stemless thistle
Carlina acaulis
'Caulescens'

**Mop-headed
hydrangea**
*Hydrangea
macrophylla*

Strawflower
*Helichrysum
bracteatum*

Nipplewort
Lapsana sp.

Bells of Ireland
or **shell flower**
Moluccella laevis

**White-flowering
hybrid tea rose**
Rosa
'Jack Frost'

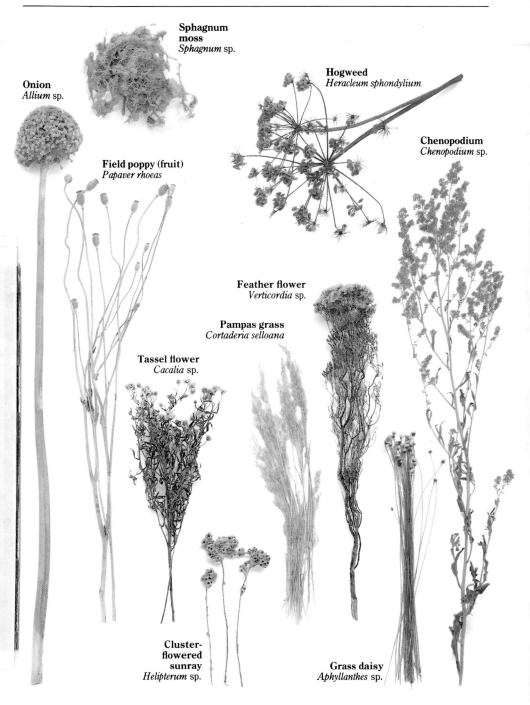

Sphagnum moss
Sphagnum sp.

Onion
Allium sp.

Hogweed
Heracleum sphondylium

Chenopodium
Chenopodium sp.

Field poppy (fruit)
Papaver rhoeas

Feather flower
Verticordia sp.

Pampas grass
Cortaderia selloana

Tassel flower
Cacalia sp.

Cluster-flowered sunray
Helipterum sp.

Grass daisy
Aphyllanthes sp.

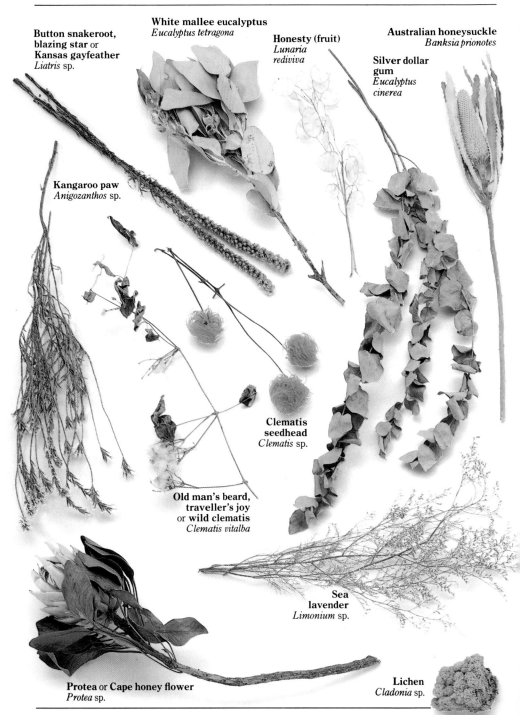

**Button snakeroot,
blazing star** or
Kansas gayfeather
Liatris sp.

White mallee eucalyptus
Eucalyptus tetragona

Honesty (fruit)
*Lunaria
rediviva*

Australian honeysuckle
Banksia prionotes

**Silver dollar
gum**
*Eucalyptus
cinerea*

Kangaroo paw
Anigozanthos sp.

**Clematis
seedhead**
Clematis sp.

**Old man's beard,
traveller's joy**
or **wild clematis**
Clematis vitalba

**Sea
lavender**
Limonium sp.

Protea or **Cape honey flower**
Protea sp.

Lichen
Cladonia sp.

Additional dried plant material

The dried plant material illustrated on the previous pages according to colour is not an exhaustive guide to the wealth of material available. The table below lists a further selection of flower and foliage that can be used successfully in dried arrangements, with an at-a-glance colour reference to the variety of shades available, to enable you to plan your arrangements effectively.

	REDS	PINKS	ORANGES	YELLOWS	BROWNS	GREENS	BLUES	PURPLES	WHITES	CREAMS	SILVERS
Allium afflatunense Decorative onion		•									
Alstroemeria ligtu Peruvian lily	•	•	•	•							
Amaryllis belladonna Belladonna lily	•	•							•		
Anaphalis yedoensis Pearly everlasting									•		
Anemone coronaria Anemone, windflower	•			•				•	•		
Astilbe arendsii Astilbe, goat's beard		•			•					•	
Bupleurum sp. Bupleurum						•					
Camellia japonica Camellia	•	•				•			•		
Centaurea macrocephala Large-headed centaurea			•								
Choisya ternata Mexican orange									•		
Corylus avallana contorta Corkscrew hazel					•						
Cytisus scoparius (Genista) Broom		•		•		•			•		
Dahlia sp. Pompom dahlia			•						•		
Delphinium consolida Larkspur		•						•	•		
Elaeagnus pungens Elaeagnus						•					
Eucalyptus ficifolia Bloodwood (large gumnuts)					•	•					
Gentiana sino-ornata Gentian							•				
Gomphrena globosa Globe amaranth									•		
Helleborus sp. Christmas rose, Lenten rose		•				•			•		
Iris foetidissima Stinking iris	•										
Kochia sp. Silver cypress, summer cypress											•
Lilium sp. Lily		•	•	•					•		
Magnolia sp. Magnolia		•	•						•		
Mahonia japonica Mahonia						•					
Picea pungens glauca Silver spruce											•
Polygonatum multiflorum Solomon's seal									•		
Salvia sp. Sage		•					•				
Santolina sp. Cotton lavender			•								•
Sedum spectabile Spectacular sedum		•									
Verticordia nitens Golden morrison			•								
Xanthorrhoea sp. Glasstree spears					•						
Xeranthemum sp. Common immortelle								•	•		
Zinnia elegans Zinnia	•		•	•						•	

· CHAPTER FIVE ·

PRINCIPLES OF DRIED FLOWER ARRANGING

Nature is the best guide when creating arrangements of dried flowers. There are no hard and fast rules. Plant shapes are well balanced and attractive when viewed singly or in groups. These are the shapes and groupings to bear in mind when creating arrangements. Before choosing your plant material or container, or deciding on the shape of the arrangements, it is best to consider the position the arrangement will take. How large does it need to be? Will it be seen from all sides? What sort of background will it be seen against? The container is also important. Natural and simple containers are usually suitable and often the shape and texture of the container will suggest shapes and textures for the arrangement. Dried flowers with warm, glowing colours look sumptuous in copper, brass and terracotta containers, whereas cool white and pale-coloured flowers look well in silver and stone containers.

Complementary container
This mix of many of the tones in the blue and purple range complements the spiral of blue and turquoise that twists down the trumpet-shaped vase. The flowers in this striking and rich arrangement include echinops, eryngium, statice and larkspur.

Style

Every arrangement of flowers – whether for a garland or a vase – contains a number of design elements which together create a certain style. The shape, colour and texture of the arrangement, together with the container if there is one and the situation in which the finished arrangement is placed, combine to give a total "look" or style.

The informality of dried flowers
Dried flowers have a natural and informal style of their own and however formal a shape you create, the completed arrangement will always have a sense of informality about it for the natural style of the flowers should greatly influence the style of the arrangement.

Simple arrangement for a bedroom table
This delicate trifoliate china dish holds a sea of pale blue delphinium flowers. Sand-dried pink roses and an auratum lily float nonchalantly on top. The complete arrangement is ideal for a romantic bedroom, bringing a touch of summer indoors.

It is often a good idea to emphasize the informal nature of dried flowers, and some of the most successful dried-flower arrangements are those that have the informality of a summer garden. Containers with a rustic feel to them work well with such arrangements precisely because they are close to the look of the plants themselves. Baskets of all types, wooden trugs and boxes, terracotta and stoneware bowls, ceramics with less sophisticated designs and finishes, all lend themselves to natural-looking, dried-flower arrangements.

Careful planning
Although a natural-looking arrangement might appear simple to achieve, it actually requires careful planning if it is not to look artificial. To begin with, it needs strength of line: curves must be strong and straight lines must be well defined. For the lines are the bones of the arrangement: they give the arrangement its essential shape. Whether created by the stems, the leaves

or seed-heads, or even the flowers themselves, they should be made first and the shape filled out afterwards. In this way the arrangement will be much easier to complete without spoiling the shape.

Cultivating your own style

Each of us has our own sense of style. When we open a magazine or book, certain images, colours and shapes appeal to us and we should draw upon these images when creating a dried-flower arrangement.

It is a good idea to make a note of the plants and colours that appeal to you. When you visit a garden, notice the combinations of flowers and foliage, and the shapes of the trees and shrubs that you like best. Then you can grow some of these plants yourself for drying, or buy bunches of them ready dried if you are not lucky enough to have a garden, and use them to create many different arrangements for your home – all reflecting your own sense of style.

The style of the room

Fortunately, a great many dried-flower arrangements fit in with even the most striking interior designs. The strong shapes of flowers like yarrow, the soft haze of fluffy gypsophila, the stately seed-heads of poppies and bulrushes: all these look wonderful against both the steel and glass of a cool, modern room and the warm, mellow wood of an old country house.

However, each room does have its own particular style, which might dictate a certain type of arrangement. The kitchen, a utilitarian place, is the ideal room in which to hang bunches of dried flowers from the ceiling, where they will be out of the way but will still form an attractive and eye-catching arrangement.

In the living room there is usually more space for table arrangements. Where there is a fireplace, a grand arrangement of dried flowers will cover the empty grate very attractively throughout the summer months. The bedroom generally has a softer style and so a gentler, prettier, perhaps more subdued, arrangement will probably be more in tune there.

Suiting the interior (top and above)
A strong yellow wall colour (top) inspired the arrangement for this elegant period fireplace throughout the summer. The abundant plant material includes yellow sunray, mimosa, golden yarrow and large-headed centaurea. In contrast, the striking arrangement of bamboo and hydrangea heads (above) complements the shapes and colours in a boldly decorated modern interior.

Colour

So much plant material can be preserved that the colour palette available to the dried-flower arranger is spectacular, and all the colours can be used in an infinite number of combinations to create a wide range of different effects.

Combining colours

It is a good idea to experiment with different combinations of colours in different quantities when beginning to create dried-flower arrangements, to discover which colours look best together.

In general, colours that lie near each other in the spectrum blend together to create a subdued but none-the-less attractive combination. So, red and orange blend well, likewise orange and yellow, yellow and green, green and blue, and blue and violet. Colours at one remove from each other in the spectrum also combine well, but produce a more striking result.

Using green and red
An eighteenth-century French faience plate is the inspiration for this arrangement of dark roseheads and their leaves. The addition of a brighter red rose seems to intensify the colour in all the flowers. The blue cornflowers echo those on the rim of the plate.

Red contrasts pleasantly with yellow, orange with green, yellow with blue, and green with violet.

In essence, the further apart two colours are from one another the more startling the effect they create. Consequently, combinations of red and green flowers, red and blue flowers, and orange or yellow and violet or purple flowers will create an extremely dramatic effect. In addition, combining a small quantity of one colour with a larger amount of an opposing colour intensifies the dominant colour. For example, a green arrangement appears even greener when a small amount of bright red is added.

Tones and shades

Pastel colours are simply muted tones of primary and secondary colours. If you were creating a pastel colour with paint you would add white, the colour of light, to the primary or secondary colour. Pale pink, peach and apricot, lilac, lemon and pale icy blues are all pastel colours. By adding black, the colour of darkness, to a primary or secondary colour you would create a more sombre tone, such as brown, rust, grey, navy blue or plum.

Pastel tones and shades are especially well represented in dried flowers. There are many pink flowers, ranging from bright to pale, that are extremely easy to dry. (See The Directory of Flowers and Foliage, pages 206–34.)

Choosing colours

By choosing colours that are close to each other in the spectrum you cannot really go wrong. But you will probably create a more interesting arrangement by being a bit more adventurous. Don't be afraid of mixing any colours at all, or indeed using only one colour by itself for a bold effect. Finally, consider the impact you wish to make with your finished arrangement. A large centrepiece, for example, will probably require a dramatic use of colour.

Blending warm colours (above)
This glowing combination of summer flowers features pink paeonies that have been dried chemically. These are offset by red roses, delicate bunches of silene, deeper pink onion heads and acacia foliage.

Muted harmony (below)
An elegant arrangement composed of closely related white, cream and silver tones, including carline thistles, hydrangeas, helichrysum, moluccella, gypsophila and honesty.

Choosing containers

Most dried-flower arrangements require a decorative container – a basket, a vase, a saucer, a dish, or some other receptacle. The choice of container is very important because, in a successful arrangement, container and plant material fuse to create a combined effect that is infinitely greater than that of either the flowers or the container separately. There should be a harmony of scale, shape, colour and texture between container and flowers. They should look completely natural together, as though they had always been meant for each other.

The scope for choosing containers is enormous. They need not be expensive nor need they be watertight. In fact, your home is probably full of containers that you have never thought of as being suitable for dried flower arrangements.

It is a good idea to make a collection of any containers that appeal to you, whatever their shape or size, but bear in mind that it is easier to make arrangements in containers with necks that are a little smaller than their bodies.

The less decorative a container, the bigger the variety of dried flowers you can use without the flowers clashing with the container. Since glass, metal and terracotta containers tend to be less decorative than ceramic ones, they open up a wider range of dried material for use.

The range of container materials

You should be able to find some glass containers in the kitchen – a tumbler, a jug or a bowl, for instance. All glass containers need to be lined with moss, petals or leaves, as the stems of dried flowers are not as attractive as those of their fresh counterparts.

Simple rectangular, square or cylindrical clear glass containers are the easiest to use since they are visually undemanding. Coloured glass restricts the choice of flower colour and forces you to be more inventive. Most difficult to arrange in is

Eighteenth-century box (left)
The painted paper lining of this container is so beautiful that a section is left showing. That, and the wonderfully subtle colours of the rug, made the choice of the ingredients – oats, fern, strawflowers, globe thistles and larkspur – inevitable. They are arranged informally to accentuate the natural, relaxed atmosphere of the room.

Glass for a sectional arrangement
A smooth glass cylinder exploits differences of texture. Separate portions of cinnamon, dried chestnuts, lentils, pasta, lavender, sunflower seeds and corn-on-the-cob are pressed against the glass by moss, while fir cones and poppy and love-in-the-mist seed-heads are arranged in segments on top.

sophisticated, highly reflective glass, which, like fine china and porcelain, can demand a formal arrangement.

Wooden containers are particularly useful, as the wood itself combines strongly with the feel of dried flowers. From a wide variety of possibilities, you might choose a curved, olive-wood salad bowl or a small box decorated with inlaid wood. A rough wooden box that seedlings have been grown in can be used for an arrangement that imitates a mossy field or it can be filled with low, brilliantly coloured helichrysums, their heads peeping just above its rim. Take advantage of the worn colours of old painted wood or the jewel-like colours of lacquered wood from India or Japan to create some distinctive arrangements. Baskets are also favoured for their

natural qualities. You might consider a waste-paper basket, a shopping basket, an old needlework basket, a simple bread basket or, for a floor-standing arrangement, a heavy-weight log basket.

Try cake-tins and moulds, worn copper saucepans or iron casseroles, or, at the other end of the scale, perhaps an eighteenth-century silver jug or an oval pewter and brass Art Nouveau vase.

Search out ceramic containers with interesting glazes, such as lustrous metallic, pitted or crystalline. Raid the garden for terracotta pots, especially those with a mossy surface. Terracotta saucers can be transformed into marvellous dried flower gardens. Likely candidates in the kitchen are a casserole dish, a jug or mug, a sugar bowl or maybe a teapot, unused because of a broken lid.

The garden is also the most likely source for stone containers such as urns and vases. They look splendid filled with enormous arrangements of dried flowers, the neutral colours of the stone complementing almost any colour combination of flowers and foliage.

Circular arrangements

Many types of arrangement do not need to be set in a container but are made on some sort of framework.

A circular arrangement such as a wreath can be based on either a copper-wire frame, purchased ready-made from a flower shop or some general stores, or a chicken-wire and moss frame you can build yourself (see p. 183). Alternatively, you can twist stems of woody vine, clematis, honeysuckle or actinidia, or supple twigs such as birch or willow, into a circle (see p. 184), entwining them and working in the ends so the finished frame is firm enough to be used as a base for attaching a variety of dried flowers, should you wish. In fact, if carefully done, such a stem wreath can look beautiful in its own right.

Harvest wreath
(below)
The final effect of the wreath (made in the sequence opposite) suggests the mellow warmth of autumn.

Woody vine base
(right)
Hay bunches, red roses, cornflowers, achillea and xeranthemum are bound on with raffia.

Bound-straw base
(below)
This simple circle comprises pale-pink and cream helichrysum, cornflowers and gypsophila. Generous pink ribbons provide the finishing touch.

Vine-stem circle
(right)
Entwined vine stems form the base of this whimsical wreath, decorated with rose leaves, pine cones and moss. A nest of woven hay, complete with eggs and blue-bird sentinel, nestles in part of the vine weave.

Making a small wreath

1 *Take a dry, prepared moss base (see p. 183). Wire sprigs of hops, flower-heads of ammobium, bunches of oats and single yellow roses. Cover the wired stems with gutta-percha tape (see p. 191).*

2 *Insert the stems of ammobium flowers into the base to provide the background to the wreath design, pushing each wire through the moss and bending it back into the base behind the wreath.*

3 *Choose the hanging point of the wreath and then complete the arrangement by filling in the moss areas, offsetting clumps of spiky oats and hops with roses and more ammobium.*

Plaited-straw base
(left)
A widening spray of blue and deep-pink larkspur, lavender and delicate oats falls in a semicircle, leaving part of the plait on view.

Incorporating ribbon
(below)
Pink ribbons, headed by a bow, are threaded and trailed through the vine stems of this wreath. Bunches of hydrangea, peach roses and gypsophila are wired in between the woody stems.

Sphagnum moss base
(below left)
A fan of grass stems, poppy seed-heads and leucodendron cones partially covers the green base.

Hanging arrangements

Dried-flower ropes, hanging bunches and swags can transform a room or stairwell and are ideal when decorating the house for a special occasion. Plaited ropes decorated with bunches of wired flowers and ribbon make an extremely attractive feature either side of the fireplace or along ceiling beams. A striking combination of bunches when wired together to make a globe shape and hung from the ceiling makes a truly grand centrepiece. Sturdy, chain-link swags made on a wire-and-hay base are ideal for hanging along a wall. More delicate swags made with reel wire can be hung around doors and pictures and also look lovely adorning the banisters.

Hanging spheres

A great glowing bunch, built up into a sphere of flowers and foliage, can transform a stairwell or the corner of a room. For the most striking result, choose dried materials with strong variations in texture and colour and arrange them informally.

Making a hanging sphere
1 *To create the stunning hanging sphere, opposite, you will need stub wires, a 3·5cm (1½in) curtain ring, scissors, and red bottlebrush, pink helichrysum, pink and yellow roses, green amaranthus, two varieties of bupleurum, clumps of sea lavender and* Leucodendron meridianum. *These will be arranged boldly in clumps so that there are some larger areas of just one colour. As with all arrangements, have everything ready to hand before you start.*

2 *Hang the curtain ring at a convenient working height. Wire separate bunches of each of the ingredients, leaving long wires for attaching. Wire the bunches to the ring one by one, leaving the stems to hang short of the ring.*

3 *Wire in more and more bunches, always bearing in mind where each will appear in the finished arrangement. The statice acts as the main filler while the spiky bottlebrush and the amaranthus serve to break the line of the curve.*

Completed sphere
The last stage of making this spectacular orb is to make minor rearrangements of individual bunches and then to hoist it into its final position. The curtain ring at its top centre will not be seen.

Hanging bunches

Both drying and dried flowers can look
marvellous hanging in bunches against
a wall, from a beam, or on a cupboard door.
When arranging a mixed bunch of dried
flowers to hang on a wall, consider carefully
both the scale of the bunch and the colours
you use, just as you would a painting, to
ensure that it suits its location, and becomes
an integral part of its surroundings.
Although hanging bunches look effective
alone, they also work well in combination.

Tying a mixed bunch

1 *The flowers and
grasses that make up
this sunny bunch are
cream helichrysum,
alchemilla, white
larkspur,* Helichrysum
italicum, *phalaris, dill
and green hydrangea.
Bear in mind that the
finished bunch will be
seen from below, so look
at it head-on as you
prepare it. Arrange an
initial bunch, using
clumps of each of the
longer stems in an
informal way. Tie tightly
with string well below
the flower-heads. You
can conceal the string
with ribbon when all the
ties are made.*

2 *Prepare a second,
denser bunch to
complement the first
and then tie it to the
first bunch, positioning
the flower-heads just
a little lower.*

3 *Complete the bunch
by tying in hydrangea
heads at the bottom of
the bunch and
disguising the string ties
with a bow.*

Textural bunch
It is the different textures of the flowers in this hanging bunch that make it so special. Clumps of white gypsophila accentuate groups of apricot-pink roses and spikes of Limonium suworowii. *A few stems of green amaranthus and* Limonium caspia *are balanced by the group of pink hydrangeas.*

Sunny bunch
This is the completed bunch, described in the sequence opposite – a warm and inviting addition to any room. A lemon satin bow complements the floral material and adds the finishing touch.

Flower ropes

Flower ropes can be either small, delicate affairs just a few inches long, such as a circlet for a bride, or long garlands of flowers to decorate a fireplace, table, archway or door or to entwine banisters or a balustrade. Circlets are usually made on a slender wire base (see p. 185), but for

longer, more sturdy garlands chicken wire and moss bases are frequently used (see p. 183). The flower ropes illustrated here are both nearly 1.8m (6ft) long so they make striking decorations on the grand scale. As both are more flexible than the chicken wire type, they would be particularly suited to spiralling down the poles of a marquee for a summer wedding, or hanging either side of a fireplace.

Decorating a plaited rope

1 *Complete a very thick raffia rope (see p. 185) to the length you require. Bind the ends firmly with raffia strands and trim neatly. Wire a small bunch of blue hydrangea flowers and brilliant yellow Helichrysum italicum (see p. 190). Attach the bunch close to the beginning of the plait by pushing the stub wire into the thickness of the plait, and bending back the end to secure. Wire similar bunches to attach later.*

2 *Prepare plumes of blue tear ribbon by doubling a length, wiring it as shown, and then tearing down each ribbon-end twice. Insert the wire of a ribbon plume into the plait above the flower bunch, and bend back to secure. Improve the feathery quality by pulling each section of ribbon over the back of a knife to curl it. (See the completed rope opposite.)*

Making an all-flower rope

1 *Take some red roses, pale pink larkspur and delicate bamboo,* Arundinaria nitida, *and arrange a bunch in a loose fashion to suit the wild look of the bamboo leaves. Tie the bunch with reel wire at the top of the bunched stems. Cover the knot with a few turns of wire, but do not detach the bunch from the reel at this stage.*

2 *Holding the stems firmly, bind down their length and slip the reel through the last loop of binding before pulling it tight in order to secure it.*

3 *Arrange a second bunch and position it lower than the first so their flowers partially overlap. Bind the second bunch to the first and hitch tight. (See the completed rope right.)*

Plaited rope
Flowers and ribbons are arranged in groups at intervals down the plait. Trailing ribbons were added towards the bottom of the plaited rope, and a raggedy raffia bow was attached at the top to cover the securing tie.

All-flower rope
The completed rope can be as long as you like, depending on how many bunches of flowers you bind in and where you intend the rope to hang. The informality of this rope makes it an ideal decoration for a cottage-style interior.

Swags

A swag, or festoon, of dried flowers is a flower rope designed to loop from one point to another. A series of swags is known as swagging. It is usually prepared for a special occasion, such as a party during a festive season, a wedding or a christening. Long tables covered with crisp white linen cloths and heavy with delicious food look even more wonderful with complementary swagging making soft curves along their edges. Doorways, alcoves, shelves, banister rails, fireplaces and ceiling beams, all take on a new look when decorated with these flowery festoons, whatever type you choose to make.

Making a long swag is certainly time-consuming. However, one of the great advantages of using dried flowers is that they last, and can be arranged well in advance, so there need be no last-minute panic to finish before the first guests arrive. Equally, the swags will continue to look good long after the last guests have left.

Making a swag on reel wire

1 *One way of making a swag is to attach bunches of flowers to a wire. Flowers for this swag include hydrangea florets, roses, oats and gypsophila. First unroll sufficient reel wire for the length of swag required. Tie a loop at this point but leave the reel attached to allow you to bind the bunch later. Wire the hydrangea florets and little bunches of gypsophila. Use them with the oats to make a posy, letting the oats stand a little taller. Trim any over-long stems that remain.*

2 *Place the bunch on the wire, directly on top of the loop, so that the flowers conceal it entirely. The loop will be used to fasten one end of the swag when it is completed.*

3 *Holding the bunch stems against the wire with one hand, bind the bunch firmly, using the attached reel of wire. Pass the reel under the last loop of binding and pull tight.*

4 *Make a second bunch and hold it so that it overlaps the stems of the first bunch. Bind again with the reel wire and hitch. Continue in this way until the swag is completed.*

Completed swags (below)
The reel-wire swag (top) looks very delicate in its pastel colours; it is, however, surprisingly strong. In contrast, the chain-link swag (bottom) has a rustic charm; trim the hay, if necessary, to maintain the shape of each link. Cover the untidy end of a swag with a ribbon.

Making a chain-link swag

1 *Each link uses a heavy-gauge stub wire, hay, raffia ties and the selected flowers – sea lavender, helichrysum and* Limonium sinuatum. *Loop the stub wire at one end.*

2 *Bind the hay around the stub wire, with raffia strands at 7·5cm (3in) intervals.*

3 *Bend the bound wire into an oval, threading the other end of the wire through the loop. Twist the wire to secure the join, cover with raffia and tidy the ends.*

4 *Decorate the ring with the flowers, tucking their stems under the raffia ties. Make as many unjoined links as necessary. Thread and join each oval through the preceding one to create the chain.*

Covering a ceiling with flowers

The inspiration for decorating a ceiling with bunches of dried flowers is the beautiful sight of cut flowers hanging to dry. If the room or corridor ceiling you have in mind has good drying conditions (see p. 198), you might indeed use fresh-cut bunches that will dry and then become a permanent decoration. For drying purposes, however, fresh-cut bunches must be separate from one another to allow the air to circulate between them, so you will not achieve the massed effect of the tight-packed dried bunches in the arrangement, below, while they are drying. The ceiling you use must be high enough to carry the dried flowers above head height. If it is too low, consider restricting the arrangement to a corner over a piece of furniture, such as a desk or side-table. If you intend decorating an entire ceiling, you can use garden wire strung between screw-eyes to support the bunches – the wire will be hidden by the final arrangement. Where the hanging will show, consider using bamboo or brass poles, iron pipes or perhaps even iron chains from which to hang the bunches.

To decorate a whole ceiling
Secure screw-eyes in opposite walls 15cm (6in) from the ceiling, at 25cm (10in) intervals, and stretch strong, plastic-coated garden wire between each pair of opposing eyes. Arrange bunches of flowers and tie them 5cm (2in) or so from the ends of the stems. The wires are gradually hidden by the hanging bunches. A great mix of colours usually works well, but the best results are achieved by arranging the bunches to vary form and texture, as well as colour.

Creating large-scale wall arrangements

Placing groups of bunches or wreaths on a wall brings a special dimension to hanging dried flowers. If you have the space you can construct a complex wall hanging. The one shown below has the overlapping, massed effect of a ceiling full of hanging bunches, but flattened into two dimensions. It has the same visual interest as a rare rug or a tapestry but brings a little of the natural world indoors.

Against a white wall, the rich and varied colours and textures of dried flowers can be displayed delightfully. If you plan to make a wall arrangement against a coloured background, choose the ingredient colours carefully, bearing in mind always that they must not only combine with each other, but also suit the background colour.

To make a wall frame
Fix hooks in the wall firmly, 1.5m (5ft) apart, to coincide with the top edge of the flower panel. Hang a length of chain from each of these so that you can slot

1.8m (6ft) bamboo poles through the links to form hanging rails. Compose your arrangement on the floor before tying the bunches to the poles on the wall. Make sure that the bunches conceal the chains.

· CHAPTER SIX ·

FLOWERCRAFT IDEAS

Dried or preserved flower decorations do not have to be arrangements of stems in containers. All the ideas in this section exploit other ways of enjoying the beauty of flowers – and not just their appearance.

In making crystallized flowers or pot-pourri, for instance, their scent is of the same or even greater importance. The delight of slipping between cool linen sheets scented with cedar and sandalwood pot-pourri never seems to pall.

Equally, all of these suggestions would make wonderful gifts for friends and other loved ones. And, with a little imagination and planning, you can create a keepsake which will recall a memory you share.

A posy or a group of pressed flowers, mounted and framed, could recapture the seasonal joys of a garden you both love, perhaps, or a summer holiday you enjoyed together. A dried-flower tree could embody some mutual flight of fantasy.

Dried flower gifts
Not only do dried flowers make special presents as arrangements, they also lend themselves to decorating and perfuming other gifts. Try making linen sachets and pot-pourri, or a herb pillow, scented and decorated candles, or jars and boxes of pot-pourri, perhaps decorated with pressed flowers. Use pressed flowers and foliage too to decorate greetings cards.

Posies

Posies are not only one of the simplest arrangements of flowers to form, they can also make beautiful presents. Unlike the more conventional fan-shaped, flat-backed bouquet, posies have a circular head of flowers arranged to be seen from every side and most commonly from above. They can also be made to look formal or shaped in a more relaxed style.

When choosing plant material for a posy it is a good idea to combine a variety of colours and textures so that the bunch can either be kept intact or split up for use in other arrangements. Dried material should be used which is bound in stem by stem. Offsetting rounded flowers with spiky material makes an attractive, eye-catching posy. Keeping a sense of scale in your arrangement is crucial: the most successful posies are compact and delicate. The flowers must not be too large and, if you are including foliage, it also should be small.

Making a posy

1 *Have ready a mixture of white larkspur, wired lilac-coloured hydrangea florets, campanula seed-heads, quaking grass and pink statice. Begin by binding just two stems together using reel wire. Add more flowers, binding them in one by one to create a curved mound. Keep the flower-heads at differing heights for an informal finished effect.*

2 *Towards completion add lower circles of flowers so that the stems are covered above the level of the wire.*

3 *Ensure that the flowers are well spaced before cutting and then tying the wire firmly. (See the completed posy opposite.)*

Making a trailing bow

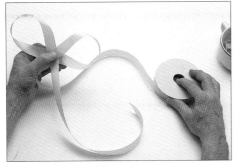

1 *Leaving a length of ribbon for one end, make a figure-of-eight. Hold the ribbon with thumb and forefinger. Allow a generous loop of ribbon, then make a second figure-of-eight on top of the first.*

2 *Leaving a similar length of ribbon for the other end, cut the ribbon. Pleat the centre of the loops between forefinger and thumb, bind the pinched underside with reel wire and knot.*

3 *Using another piece of the ribbon, bind the stems of the bunch to cover any visible wiring and tie firmly. Place the bow on top of the bound stems with the ends of the binding ribbon above and below.*

4 *Tie one bow with the ends of the binding ribbon to secure the trailing bow firmly in position. Check all ribbon ends have been cut to a similar angle and tease the completed bow into shape.*

Informal posy
This is the posy being assembled in the step-by-step sequence opposite. It has been finished with a pretty, peach-pink bow that both complements the arrangement and conceals the wiring.

Dried-flower trees

A miniature "tree" made with dried flowers can look spectacularly architectural positioned as a free-standing floor arrangement or, on a smaller scale placed on a low table top to look like a Bonsai tree.

First decide what height you want the tree, bearing in mind the objects which will surround it. Then, unless you are planning to create an artificial, primarily geometric shape, let nature be your guide when choosing the form the tree will take. It could be based on an oak tree or a conical-shaped bay tree, a conifer or an open-branched magnolia. Once you have decided on the shape and size of the tree you must decide on the container. The choice of container is very important and for the most successful effect you should select one large enough to create the impression that the tree might really be growing in it.

Mop-headed tree and copse (opposite)
Deep red helichrysum flowers and pieces of purple Celosia argentea cristata *make the mop-headed tree on the right a particularly striking example. A foam lozenge covered in golden rod impaled on several birch twigs creates the little copse on the left.*

Decorating a cone-shaped tree

1 *See page 187 for full instructions on how to make the base for this tree. Dry sphagnum moss has been pinned to cover the dry-foam base. Push dried-flower stems into the foam through the moss, firstly using alchemilla as a background, followed by red roses, wired celosia and finally fine twigs.*

2 *Wedge the inner post into the outer container and mound dry bun moss at the base of the trunk.*

Pressed flowers

Many flowers, grasses and leaves retain much of their colour and delicacy when pressed. Narcissus, scillas, primroses and snowdrops all look very attractive; so, too, do daisy-shaped flowers and the smaller stems of heucera, forget-me-not, gypsophila and crocosmia. Fleshy plants do not usually press successfully, and full-petalled flowers, such as roses and paeonies, have a tendency to look ugly because their flower-heads are too bulky and their petals overlap. However, the overlapping petals of trumpet-shaped flowers can be used to good effect to create attractive patterns.

You can make your own flower press very easily or buy one ready made. Alternatively, small pieces can be pressed between the pages of a heavy book, and larger pieces by placing them under a rug or carpet, preferably where no traffic will disturb them. Always sandwich the material between absorbent paper so that it is dried as well as pressed.

The simplest way of making your own press is to cut two pieces of plywood into rectangles about 30 × 20cm (11½ × 8in). Bore holes in the corners of each piece. Insert a bolt into each hole in one piece; wing nuts will be used to clamp the wood together when the press is filled.

The most attractive way of presenting pressed flowers is to mount and frame them. Position your material on a sheet of good quality matt card – off-white or cream is usually best. Stick each piece in position, using a latex-based adhesive, placing a tiny spot on the centre back of it, or a clear plastic adhesive spray. You must make sure that the material is positioned correctly first time, as it is difficult to move. Choose a simple frame that does not detract from the delicacy of the plants.

Arranging pressed material
This simple arrangement is given elegant form by pointing all the stems in the same direction. The mixture of colours and textures provides interest.

Sampler arrangement

A border of rose leaves frames groups of violas, lace-cap hydrangeas, cow parsley and an anemone. Rose and fern leaves make particularly effective borders, so do the silver leaves of Cineraria maritima, *and trails of small-leaved ivy can work well. Be careful not to position flowers or leaves too close to the edge of the mounting card or they may be obscured by the frame – broad margins are safest. This picture was inspired by a sampler, but botanical paintings may also stimulate ideas for your own designs. There are no hard and fast rules for designed pressed flower pictures. You could be guided by the way the plant grows, recalling the grouping of its flowers and foliage.*

Using a press

Pressing flowers with bulky centres

Place a piece of cardboard and then a folded sheet of blotting paper on the base of the press. Insert the plant material between the two "faces" of the folded blotting paper. Cover with another piece of cardboard. Continue until the press is full. The intermediate pieces of cardboard are important since they prevent plant impressions passing from layer to layer.

1 *Place a piece of cardboard and then a folded sheet of blotting paper in the press. Insert the plant material into the blotting paper, arranging it on the lower of the two "faces" and then cut holes in the upper "face" to align exactly with the centres of the flowers. Close the sheet of blotting paper, covering the petals. The centres of the flowers will poke through the holes.*

2 *Cut a thin slice of foam to the same thickness as the centres of the flowers. Cut holes in it which will align with the flower centres and place the foam on top of the folded sheet of blotting paper. The flower centres should now be level with the top of the foam. Place a piece of cardboard carefully on top of foam and then continue loading the press, layering the material.*

Pot-pourri

Rose petals, lavender, mimosa, pinks, lilies, jasmine, violets and honeysuckle all retain their perfume for a long time after drying. While a mixture of such scented flowers alone will emit a delicate fragrance, a more pervasive perfume is achieved by adding herbs, spices, seeds, bark, oil and fixatives to make pot-pourri.

There are two methods of making pot-pourri: the dry and the moist. Whichever you choose, the flowers should be picked as the buds open, preferably on a dry day after any dew has evaporated.

The moist method The plant material is partly dried on sheets of absorbent material, such as blotting paper. After two days, when the petals have shrunk, all the plant material is placed in a jar in alternate layers of salt. The mixture is stirred every day for two weeks, by which time it should be crumbly. A fixative, such as orris root or tonka beans, and spices and essential oils are added and the jar sealed. The contents are then left for about six weeks to mature.

The dry method The plant material is dried completely (this takes ten days or more, depending on its density), then mixed with fixative, spices and oils, and placed in a jar to mature. The jar is sealed and shaken every day for about six weeks until ready for use.

Put pot-pourris in small bowls and place them around the house. To make them especially decorative, add some large, colourful dried-flower petals. Pot-pourris will scent the air for many months, and even then the perfumes can be reawakened with essential oils.

Cottage garden mix

Lavender mix

Spicy mix

Spring mix

RECIPE INGREDIENTS

Spring mix (dry method)
1 cup each: lemon-scented geranium leaves, lemon verbena leaves, mimosa flowers, myrtle leaves
Grated peel 2 lemons
¼ cup orris powder
4 drops each: citronella, rose geranium oil

Cottage garden mix (moist method)
5 cups scented pink rose petals
2 cups each: marigolds, paeony petals
1 cup each: bergamot flowers, honeysuckle flowers, scented pinks
4 cups natural salt
½ cup allspice
⅓ cup orris powder
6 drops each: rose oil, rose geranium oil, bergamot oil

Lavender mix (dry method)
3 cups lavender flowers
2 cups pale pink rose leaves

1 cup each: lemon balm leaves, leptospermum leaves, sweet woodruff
Grated peel 2 lemons
¼ cup orris powder
4 drops lavender oil

Spicy mix (moist method)
1 cup each: juniper berries, bay berries, myrtle cones, sandalwood cones, Jerusalem thorn, rose hips, bergamot flowers, rose petals
2 tbsp each: ground cinnamon, cloves
1 cup natural salt
½ cup each: sliced ginger root, pounded allspice, anise seeds, red lichen, patchouli
Grated peel 3 oranges and 3 limes

Fragrant garden mix (moist method)
2 cups each: pale pink rose petals, lime blossoms, white lilac flowers
1 cup each: philadelphus flowers,

lily-of-the-valley flowers, lippia leaves, chamomile flowers, white dianthus flowers, myrtle leaves, rose geranium leaves
4 cups natural salt
6 drops verbena oil
4 drops lily-of-the-valley oil
30g (1oz) gum benzoin

Rose mix (dry method)
8 cups dried red rose petals
1 tbsp ground cloves
2 tbsp each: ground allspice, cinnamon, orris
4 drops rose oil

Woody mix (dry method)
4 cups cedar twigs
2 cups cedar bark shavings
1 cup sandalwood shavings
2 tbsp orris powder
4 drops each: cedarwood oil, sandalwood oil

Fragrant garden mix

Rose mix

Woody mix

Crystallized flowers

Crystallized flowers are easy to prepare and, as well as looking beautiful, they are delicious to eat. Almost any flowers can be crystallized, the best ones being violets, primroses and scented rose petals, while citrus blossom is a must. Because scented flowers retain much of their perfume when they are crystallized they are especially good to eat. Cherry, apple and pear blossom are all fragrant tasting, as are acacia and elderflower.

Crystallized leaves can look extremely attractive too, especially when used to make a border on top of a cake. A rich chocolate cake with fresh mint icing and filling is made all the more luscious by the addition of a border of crystallized mint leaves. Lemon balm leaves and scented geranium leaves are excellent for this purpose, too. Slices of angelica stalk (*Angelica archangelica*) are delicious when crystallized.

It is, of course, important to make quite sure that the plants you choose are not poisonous. In addition, when choosing flowers, make sure that they are of a scale to suit the dish you plan to decorate. It is a common mistake to use flowers or leaves that are too large.

Gum arabic or egg white

There are two methods of crystallizing: in one you use gum arabic to preserve the plant material and in the other you use egg white. Flowers and leaves crystallized using gum arabic last for a long time. You can buy chocolates decorated with violets or rose petals that have been crystallized in this way.

If you wish the plant material to last for many months you should use gum arabic. Dissolve 12g (½oz) gum arabic in ¼ cup of cold water in a double boiler or in a basin placed in a pan of simmering water. Stir until dissolved, then remove from the heat and allow the solution to cool. While it is cooling, make a syrup with ¼ cup of water and 100g (4oz) sugar. Boil to 80°C (176°F), then remove the pan from the heat and allow to cool.

Apply the gum arabic solution to both sides of the leaves or petals of the flowers with a paintbrush. Next, brush on the sugar solution. Finally, sift caster sugar over the plant material, using a teaspoon to ensure that it is completely coated. Allow to dry on greaseproof paper.

Flowers crystallized using egg white look more beautiful than those crystallized using gum arabic, but they will not last long and should be eaten within four or five days. However, as the life of a cake or tart is fairly short, this should not present a problem. To crystallize using egg white, follow the step-by-step illustrations given opposite.

Fragrant taste of flowers (left)
This deliciously cool looking iced sponge cake is decorated with crystallized leaves and flowers, prepared using the egg-white method. The sweet-scented violets, little blue borage flowers and yellow-centred auricula are edible but the pretty, heart-shaped violet leaves are simply for decoration.

Crystallizing with egg white

1 *Beat the white of an egg lightly until it is of a frothing and even consistency. Using a paintbrush, very gently cover the petals of the flower with the beaten egg white, making sure that you give an even but light coating to both the upper and the lower surfaces. It is very important to make sure that you do not overwet the petals.*

2 *Sprinkle caster sugar carefully all over the flower, making sure that there is an even coverage. Shake off any excess sugar so the flowers are still visible through the coating. Place the flowers on a cake rack covered with greaseproof paper and leave in a warm place. The egg white will dry in a couple of hours.*

*Crystallized flower-head of the common camellia (*Camellia japonica *'Adolphe Anderson').*

· CHAPTER SEVEN ·

DRIED
FLOWERS FOR
SPECIAL
OCCASIONS

Life would be very dull without special
occasions. The seasonal festivals –
Christmas, Easter and Harvest or
Thanksgiving – bring a shape and form to
the year and in between there are
birthdays, weddings and christenings. All
of them afford us the chance to celebrate,
which is what life is really about. And
where there is celebration, there should
be flowers.

If you are using only dried flowers for any
of these occasions, you will have one great
advantage over the fresh-flower arranger:
you can prepare such decorations well in
advance. This is invaluable if you know you
will have hundreds of last-minute things
to organize.

The arrangements that are included in this
section can all be adapted to your own
particular celebrations. Let them act as a
springboard for your own designs.

Birthday basket
*A woody basket, fragrant with pot-pourri (see
pp. 158–9), is filled with red roses, poppies, pink
larkspur, Chinese lanterns, safflowers and Alchemilla
mollis to create a truly sumptuous present. Wrapping
it in cellophane and adding red and pink satin
ribbons completes what would make a wonderful gift
in the depths of winter.*

Valentine's Day

The first Valentine cards date from the very beginning of the British postal system in the sixteenth century, when elaborate lace-paper cards were produced complete with verses. You could make your own Valentine card simply by writing a verse on a piece of plain card and mounting a border of pressed flowers, such as violets or primroses, on to it.

The red rose has long been a symbol of true love and is now associated with Valentine's Day. This is a more recent innovation, of course, as in colder climates roses are not in flower at this time of year and until recently were available out of season only at great expense.

However, roses dry very well, and red roses keep their intense rich colour for many months if they are dried correctly. Attaching a single bloom to a present makes a poignant memento. Alternatively, an arrangement of dried flowers containing some red roses, like the heart illustrated here, is a loving present.

Making a heart of red roses

1 *Make one large 2.5cm (1in) diameter moss-filled, chicken-wire tube 1m 15cm (3ft 9in) long and two thinner tubes, one 38cm (15in) and the other 10cm (4in) long (see p. 183). Bend the large tube into a heart shape and join the ends at the top with mossing wire. Using the same wire, bind on the silver-sprayed heather, overlapping each previous piece to cover the whole frame.*

2 *Take the 38cm (15in) tube and set the 10cm (4in) tube at right angles to one end. Bind the two together with mossing wire to make a "T" shape. Bend the shorter tube to form the arrow-head point.*

3 *Divide the silver-sprayed sedge into small bunches. Bind the shortest to the top of the shaft with wire and continue down two-thirds of the shaft. Bind two bunches to the head with raffia.*

Valentine heart
A heart of red roses makes a very special Valentine's Day present in true Victorian style. Silver-sprayed tree heather covers the heart-shaped base while the arrow is bound with small-headed sedge. This arrangement used 80 red roses.

4 *Feed the shaft diagonally through the heart from the back until the head protrudes by 5–7.5cm (2–3in). Tie the shaft to the heart just under the head and near the shaft end, using mossing wire. Attach a silver ribbon bow to the shaft to cover the last wire tie.*

5 *Decorate the heart with roses, their stems trimmed to 3.5cm (1½in) long and a razor-sharp angle. Take care to space them evenly around the heart shape. Check that they are firmly in position, then cut off any protruding stems.*

Wedding Day

This day, one of the most important in many people's lives, is strongly associated with flowers. Although fresh flower bouquets look wonderful, sadly they soon wilt and die. Dried flowers, on the other hand, can be kept for many years as a keepsake. Another great advantage with dried flowers is that all the arrangements can be made in your own time, if necessary weeks in advance.

It is important to establish a colour theme for the flower decorations. This does not mean that the same flowers need to be used in all the arrangements, just that the colours and general textures should match. Although an all-white wedding is beautiful, it is now more usual to mix white and cream or other pastel-coloured flowers or use multi-coloured mixes.

The bride's bouquet can be made to many different designs. The most important point is to make sure that the flowers are easy to hold and that the bouquet is scaled to look important but not overpowering. Nowadays, bouquets are rarely longer than 45cm (18in), shaped like a tear drop, and vary in style between very formal and very wild. Some brides prefer to carry a posy, and there is also the option of carrying a beautiful bunch cradled in the arm. For bridesmaids, a posy is ideal.

For the wedding reception there is nothing like rich garlands and swags to add atmosphere. Used to decorate buffet tables or the poles of a marquee, their handsome impact is well worth the effort involved. Arrangements can also be prepared for pedestals and table tops.

Pedestal arrangement for a reception
The flowers (many extended, see p. 189) in this soft colour mix are helipterum, kangaroo paw, gypsophila, wild bamboo, Stachys lanata, and fine grass and banksia foliage. The reconstituted stone urn contains a bucket with foam piled 20cm (8in) above its rim.

Making a spray bouquet

1 *Wire and cover every stem to be used. Make a flat-backed spray, three-quarters the length of the bouquet, binding each piece in with reel wire. Cover the wires with gutta-percha tape.*

2 *Continue to bind in pieces of plant material, fanning out the shape until they "trail" to a length that you judge is sufficient. Bend the stems as you go to form the handle which the bride will hold.*

3 *Bind in more stems to form a posy shape above the trail. Wired stems make arrangement very easy. Cut and tie the reel wire and trim the handle of the bouquet to 17.5cm (7in).*

4 *Make a trailing ribbon bow (see p. 153) and, using the same kind of ribbon, bind down the handle, leaving an end to tie.*

5 *Continue binding to the end of the handle and back. Knot the ribbon ends and use the ends to tie on the bow.*

Casual elegance (right)
When complete, the spray bouquet is a formal arrangement, although its outline is deliberately irregular.

Ready for the celebrations (right)

Swags of flowers have been tacked to the edge of the wedding-cake table, with glossy trailing bows added to cover the joins. The cake is encircled with a single row of helichrysum and rose heads, and a small arrangement decorates the top. Beside the cake is the bride's bouquet and on the chair, in front of the pedestal, are the bride's head-dress and bridesmaid's posy. A posy can be carried by a bridesmaid of any age. For a very young girl, a little basket of flowers would be a perfect solution, as it is small, light and easy to hold. A pretty little sphere of flowers would be a popular choice for 5–10-year-olds.

Bridal bouquet (above)

This simple bunch arrangement is made with flowers which match the other floral decorations, including bright pink roses, gypsophila, pale creamy pink helichrysum, yellow kangaroo paw, oats and some feathery foliage. Use the longest stems first and make absolutely sure that all the thorns are removed from the rose stems before you begin.

Harvest time and Thanksgiving

Autumn comes and with it sadness at the loss of the long and easy summer days, but also a sense of something gained. As the crops are gathered in, as the evenings become colder, it is the time to give thanks for all that nature supplies – an ideal time for a party.

It is also an ideal time for dried flowers. The bunches that were gathered in summer and early autumn are dry and ready to be used, and the autumn spectrum of colours – glowing golds, rusts and oranges – are a joy to arrange. Think of the warmth of brightly coloured flowers like deep red pom-pom dahlias, golden rod, brilliant orange Chinese lanterns and the many colours of hydrangeas. Consider too field cereals, wild grasses and seed-heads.

Shops and markets at this time are full of fruits and vegetables with the same glowing colours – red apples, golden pears, gourds – and there is no reason why you should not mix these with dried flowers both in arrangements and in swags and garlands. Use nature's wealth to welcome your friends with a display which celebrates the year's harvest.

Welcoming hallway (below)
The swagging around the doorway frames a matching wreath on the door based on a circle of twisted vine stems (see p. 184). A splendid barley sheaf stands to the left of the door. On the right a two-tier table is decorated above with a chubby golden gourd, a mug filled with dried barley, grasses and Chinese lanterns and a hay-covered cornucopia (see p. 181), and below with several smaller arrangements.

Making the harvest swag

1 *Use a hay-filled roll of chicken-wire for the swag base (see p. 183); it may be necessary to join several to achieve the required length. Wire bunches of Chinese lanterns, barley and hay (see p. 190). Wire fresh apples through their cores, bend over the end of the emerging wire and then pull it back into the core.*

2 *Push heavy-gauge stub wire into the stem of each corn head and wind it around the stem to secure. Cover all wires with gutta-percha tape (see p. 178). Arrange bunches of plant material along the swag, each overlapping the last, and twist the wires into the base. Wire in corn heads and apples at intervals.*

Making a sheaf

Take a generous bunch of black-eared barley and, using three-quarters of it, make a central core of stems, building up gradually, adding layer on layer and binding each layer with string. Use the final quarter of stems to form an outer layer, securing it to the inner core with a single binding positioned high up the stems so that they splay sideways in a spiral. Trim the stalk ends carefully and the central column will act as a pedestal. Add a plaited raffia circlet to cover the binding (see p. 185). Seeding grasses, rushes, cereals and reeds should be picked at their prime. They are all easy to dry and can be either laid flat on paper or left standing in vases without water.

Christmas

Christmas, or Christ's Mass, has been celebrated as the birth of Christ on 25 December since the early part of the fourth century AD. Before that the Emperor Aurelian chose 25 December as the birthday of the unconquered sun and, to this day, Christmas contains elements of the winter rites linked with the solar calendar called the Kalends.

When we decorate houses with greenery and coloured lights and exchange presents we are performing part of the ancient pagan rites. In fact, that most pagan of all plants, mistletoe, was allowed into the home and the Church only after Pope Gregory I agreed that pagan customs should be assimilated into Christianity.

Dried flowers can be used in Christmas decorations to stunning effect either on their own or mixed with fresh greenery such as pine, yew and holly. Many varieties of conifer such as blue pine, Scots pine and Irish yew, dry well.

If you use dried flowers mixed with the foliage from one or more conifers, you have the advantage that you can make your Advent wreaths, basket arrangements, garlands and even trees well in advance of Christmas in the knowledge that they will last throughout the whole of the festive season. But if you wish to make some garlanding using dried material and the bright red berries and rich green foliage of holly, add the holly just before Christmas as both its leaves and berries will soon wilt in a warm room.

Christmas colour

Brightly coloured dried flowers, such as Chinese lantern, red helichrysum, red roses and bottlebrush, look dashing against the dark rich greens of Christmas trees and foliage. So, too, do the ice-cool whites, silvers and pale blues of gypsophila and larkspur, helichrysum, senecio and santolina foliage, and hydrangea and pale blue larkspur. Anything goes when you are decorating a tree and a great mixture of

flowers and colours always looks wonderful. However, a tree decorated in one or two colours, perhaps red and green, pink and silver or orange and gold, can look as stunning as one bedecked with every colour under the sun.

Ropes of dried flowers and foliage will brighten the house during the Christmas season. Fireplaces, doorways and staircases, tables, shelves and pictures are given new life when surrounded by garlanding (see pp. 146–7 for techniques). Using rich green foliage provides an added brilliance, but ropes made entirely from dried material can also be stunning and dried-flower ropes too can be made at your leisure, well before Christmas.

Cool, elegant tree (above and opposite)
Silver-sprayed baskets filled with dried hydrangea heads (see the detail above) and crisp, white, dried gypsophila dusted with glitter adorn this unusual and charming tree. Other tree decorations from dried flowers can be equally effective. Stick together groups of four or five bright-coloured helichrysum heads to form small spheres and hang them beside the more traditional glass and paper decorations. Little posies of multi-coloured flowers also look very attractive.

Dramatic swagging (above)
The asymmetric swagging over the hearth dominates this interior. Two swags were made, each by overlapping a series of bunches (see p. 146). The plant material includes dried pine branches, *helichrysum, twigs with silver-glittered cones, leptospermum and fresh, variegated holly. The flower-pot arrangement on the hearth is a chicken-wire sphere (see p. 186) covered with dyed-green lichen and dotted with bright red berries on wires.*

Festive wreath
(above)
*Three branches of blue
spruce, each 60cm (2ft)
long, and some silver-
coned twigs form the
basis of this wreath,
decked with helichrysum
clusters and pink
spheres. Ribbons cascade
from a bow covering
the tie.*

**Tea caddy
arrangement**
(above right)
*Twigs and eucalyptus
leaves were sprayed with
silver paint and glitter
dust for a festive look.*

Formal centrepiece
(right)
*A massed chicken-wire
base (see p. 183) is
decorated with clematis
seed-heads, roses,
helichrysum, green
hydrangeas, lichen
and agonis and
asmunda fern.*

· CHAPTER EIGHT ·

TOOLS, MATERIALS AND TECHNIQUES

The tools and materials required for
making fresh- and dried-flower
arrangements are few and simple. All you
need is shown in this section, together
with the necessary, though straight-
forward, techniques you should master to
be sure of a professional finish to your
work, whether in containers or on bases.
Become proficient at these techniques
and you will be able to tackle all the
arrangements shown in this book and feel
confident of making up your own
creations for all sorts of occasions.
The following pages also contain
the practical details of air drying fresh
flowers, drying with desiccants,
preserving with glycerine and colouring
plant material, as well as how to store
plant material once it has been dried.

An ideal workspace
*Few of us can enjoy the luxury of a room set apart
for conditioning, arranging, drying and storing
flowers and foliage, but with imagination it is possible
to make use of smaller spaces. For instance, a prettily
painted hanging cupboard placed in a hall or
stairway could easily be fitted out for storing dried
flowers and other plant materials. Make sure the
cupboard is well ventilated.*

Tools and materials

There is a very wide range of equipment available to the professional flower arranger, but many items are useful only on the odd occasion. Set out below are the materials and tools used for the arrangements in this book. The essential items are high-quality florist's scissors, a tough steel knife and some foam. The others are regularly useful and can be purchased at many flower shops or stores.

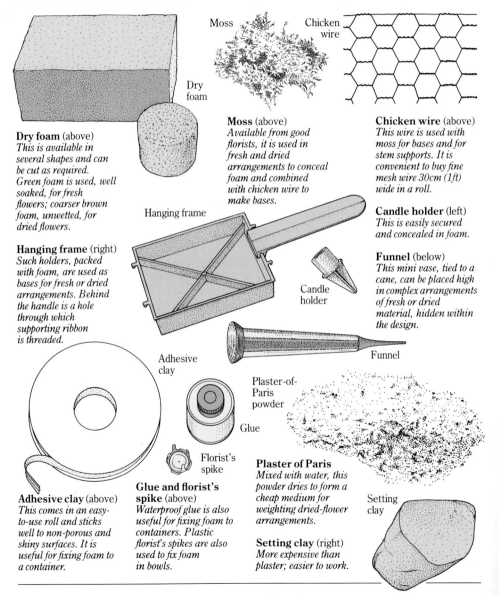

Moss

Chicken wire

Dry foam

Dry foam (above)
This is available in several shapes and can be cut as required. Green foam is used, well soaked, for fresh flowers; coarser brown foam, unwetted, for dried flowers.

Moss (above)
Available from good florists, it is used in fresh and dried arrangements to conceal foam and combined with chicken wire to make bases.

Chicken wire (above)
This wire is used with moss for bases and for stem supports. It is convenient to buy fine mesh wire 30cm (1ft) wide in a roll.

Candle holder (left)
This is easily secured and concealed in foam.

Hanging frame

Hanging frame (right)
Such holders, packed with foam, are used as bases for fresh or dried arrangements. Behind the handle is a hole through which supporting ribbon is threaded.

Funnel (below)
This mini vase, tied to a cane, can be placed high in complex arrangements of fresh or dried material, hidden within the design.

Candle holder

Funnel

Adhesive clay

Plaster-of-Paris powder

Glue

Florist's spike

Adhesive clay (above)
This comes in an easy-to-use roll and sticks well to non-porous and shiny surfaces. It is useful for fixing foam to a container.

Glue and florist's spike (above)
Waterproof glue is also useful for fixing foam to containers. Plastic florist's spikes are also used to fix foam in bowls.

Plaster of Paris
Mixed with water, this powder dries to form a cheap medium for weighting dried-flower arrangements.

Setting clay

Setting clay (right)
More expensive than plaster; easier to work.

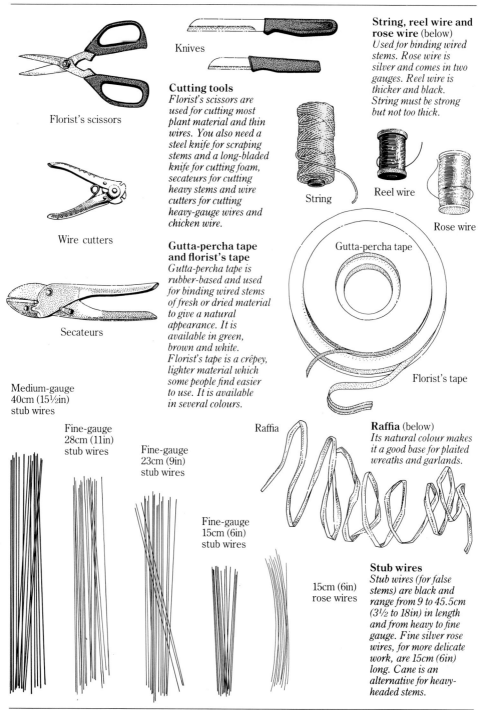

Knives

Cutting tools
Florist's scissors are used for cutting most plant material and thin wires. You also need a steel knife for scraping stems and a long-bladed knife for cutting foam, secateurs for cutting heavy stems and wire cutters for cutting heavy-gauge wires and chicken wire.

Florist's scissors

Wire cutters

Secateurs

String, reel wire and rose wire (below)
Used for binding wired stems. Rose wire is silver and comes in two gauges. Reel wire is thicker and black. String must be strong but not too thick.

String

Reel wire

Rose wire

Gutta-percha tape and florist's tape
Gutta-percha tape is rubber-based and used for binding wired stems of fresh or dried material to give a natural appearance. It is available in green, brown and white. Florist's tape is a crêpey, lighter material which some people find easier to use. It is available in several colours.

Gutta-percha tape

Florist's tape

Medium-gauge 40cm (15½in) stub wires

Fine-gauge 28cm (11in) stub wires

Fine-gauge 23cm (9in) stub wires

Fine-gauge 15cm (6in) stub wires

Raffia

Raffia (below)
Its natural colour makes it a good base for plaited wreaths and garlands.

15cm (6in) rose wires

Stub wires
Stub wires (for false stems) are black and range from 9 to 45.5cm (3½ to 18in) in length and from heavy to fine gauge. Fine silver rose wires, for more delicate work, are 15cm (6in) long. Cane is an alternative for heavy-headed stems.

Preparing containers

Although it is not necessary to prepare every single container for displaying flowers – natural-looking arrangements can look stunning arranged nonchalantly in a jug – flower arranging is often much simpler if the stems are held in supporting material.

Foam (see p. 178) is the most efficient supporting material. It is easy to sculpt and, if your container is especially large, you can always bind two pieces together and fix both to the bottom on florist's spikes (see p. 178). If you are preparing a fresh-flower arrangement, make sure that the foam is thoroughly soaked before you use it and fill the container with water once the arrangement is complete. If your container

has incurving sides, chicken wire might be a good alternative, and, for a simple arrangement in a glass container, marbles or pebbles will hold stems in position.

If you are preparing a glass container with wet foam and you wish to conceal it, simply surround it with moss: it loves the water. The stems of dried material are generally unattractive and look particularly ugly seen through the sides of a glass vase. This problem is easily overcome by lining the inside of the container – between glass and foam – with pot-pourri or moss.

Some containers will require lining before you fill them with water! Others will need to be adapted or decorated.

Preparing a ceramic container

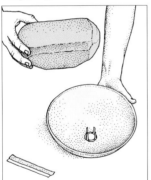
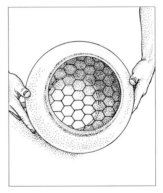

Far left: For a bowl which curves outwards, secure foam sculpted to fit to a florist's spike fixed to the bottom of the bowl with adhesive clay. To prepare a shallow, saucer-shaped container, stick a sculpted mound of foam to the base with glue (a waterproof type if preparing a fresh arrangement).

Left: As an alternative to a foam support for a container which curves inwards, you can stretch a piece of chicken wire inside the rim and pull it upwards until it grips the lipped sides.

Lining a porous container for fresh flowers

1 *Place a non-porous bowl of appropriate size inside the container. You may need to pack the space between basket and container with foam. Fix a florist's spike to the bottom of the bowl with adhesive clay.*

2 *Using a sharp knife, sculpt a piece of wet foam to fit the bowl and fix it securely to the florist's spike on the base of the bowl.*

3 *Insert damp moss to conceal packing between the sides of the container and bowl, if necessary, and also on top of the wet foam.*

Preparing a glass container

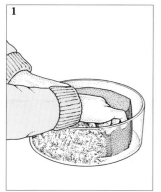

1 *Fix two florist's spikes to the bottom of the container with adhesive clay. Sculpt a block of foam, wet if arranging fresh flowers, to fit neatly inside the container.*

2 *Secure the foam on the florist's spikes in the centre of the container. Surround and cover the foam with clumps of damp moss. If using taller cylinder shapes for dried-flower arrangements, pressed autumnal leaves placed between glass and moss look good.*

Decorating a container with paper

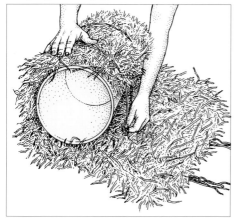

Glue scraps of colourful paper to the inside of the clear container, overlapping each piece with the next to create a "mosaic" effect. Varnish to prevent the paper from peeling. Place a lining vase inside the decorated container.

Adapting a wastepaper basket

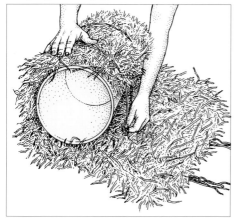
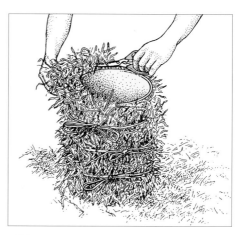

1 *Place two strands of raffia on the floor, and cover with a thick layer of hay. Roll the wastepaper basket carefully over the hay, using the raffia to hold it in place around the sides of the container.*

2 *Tie the ends of the raffia into bows, and add further ties if necessary to secure the hay in place. Trim untidy sections with scissors. (See the wicker horn-shape covered in this way on p. 171.)*

Preparing bases

A chieving a professional and satisfying result when arranging flowers involves good groundwork. Time spent preparing saves arranging time later on. This includes time spent making your own wreath, sphere and tree bases if you want an alternative to shop-bought varieties.

Shop-bought bases are usually made from plastic and dry foam, but wire frames of various types are commercially available and these you can cover with moss. It is even more satisfying to make your own frame, using one of the methods shown, as you have full control of its design.

We know from paintings and sculptures that wreaths (rigid circles of flowers and/or foliage) have been traditional wall or door decorations since early times, especially wreaths of sweet-smelling flowers and aromatic herbs. There are several different methods of making bases for circular arrangements. You can weave supple stems together to form a frame or roll chicken wire around sphagnum moss to form a long sausage and sew the ends together to make a circle. Chicken wire is very useful for flower arrangers: it can also be used (with foam) for the base of a dried-flower sphere or for thick garlands and swags of fresh or dried plant material. For a delicate circlet of dried flowers stub wire (see p. 179) is all you need to make a base.

Making bases for wreaths, spheres and ornamental trees entails using damp or sappy plant material which must be left to dry thoroughly before it is used with dried flowers or your arrangement will quickly spoil. Drying can take up to a week.

Covering a shop-bought wire frame

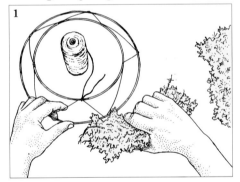

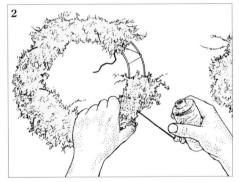

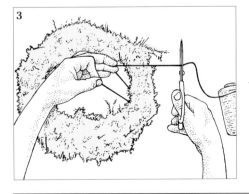

1 To a shop-bought wire frame, tie the end of a reel of string, leaving a short length beyond the knot. Take a small clump of damp moss.

2 Holding the moss against the frame, bind it on securely with the string. Continue binding around the frame, overlapping the clumps.

3 Overlap the last clump of moss with the first and bind it in. Cut the string and tie the end to the original knot end to make a neat finish. Let the moss dry thoroughly before using dried flowers.

Making a circular moss and chicken wire base

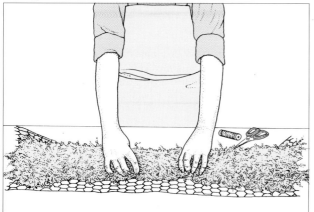

1 *Cut a piece of 30cm (1ft) chicken wire to the length of the circumference you want. Lay it flat, and arrange damp sphagnum moss along one edge. Roll the wire tightly over the moss to form a solid tube approximately 7cm (3in) thick. Tuck in the moss and turn in any sharp wires as you roll.*

2 *Bend the tube round evenly to form a circle, gradually curving it to keep the circle smooth. Do not overlap the ends; these will be sewn together neatly.*

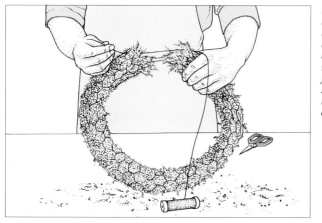

3 *Attach reel wire to one end of the chicken wire tube, leaving a loose end for finishing. Sew the two ends of the tube together, and tie and conceal the wire ends. Sphagnum moss is commercially available, from any good florist or store. Remember to let it dry out thoroughly before use if making a dried-flower arrangement.*

Making a stem circle

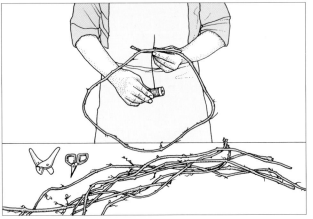

1 *The stems of various climbing plants and certain particularly supple tree branches can be used to make wreath bases. The stems must be supple and cut into wands roughly 1.3m (4½ft) long. The stems of the vine* Actinidia chinesis *and branches of willow and birch make particularly handsome bases. Make a circle of the required size with one wand of your chosen material and secure it firmly with reel wire.*

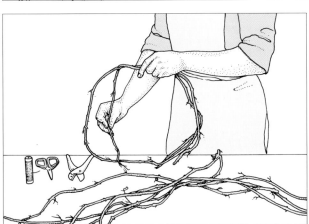

2 *Take another wand, engage it near the binding, and then twine it carefully round the first ring and secure the end firmly.*

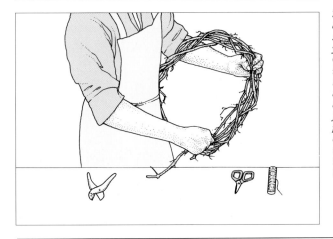

3 *Continue to wind in the lengths of plant material, allowing oddly shaped wands to create holes, until you reach the thickness you require. Cut away the wire once the circle is self supporting. If the base is to be used for a dried-flower arrangement, leave it to dry out completely before attaching any flowers. A wreath need not be packed with material around its entire circumference. A stem circle is decorative, and you can allow it to show through, or leave a portion bare for a dynamic effect.*

Making a delicate circlet

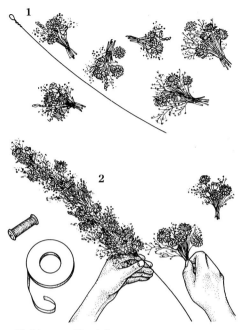

1 *Make small bunches of ingredients. Join two stub wires, twisting an "eye" in one end and trimming the other to 5cm (2in) longer than the circumference of the head. Cover with gutta-percha tape.*

2 *Bind on the bunches using reel wire, covering each binding with tape. Hide the "eye" with the first bunch and the stems of each bunch with the flowers of the next. Leave 2.5cm (1in) of wire free.*

3 *Bend the decorated wire into a circle. Thread the free wire through the "eye" and bend it back to secure. The flowers of the first bunch on the stub wire should cover the stems of the last bunch.*

Making a raffia plait

1 *Attach a good bunch of raffia strands, as thick as the required base, to a firm support. Divide the raffia into three equal portions and weave the left portion and then the right portion alternately over the central portion until you reach the end of the strands. Bind the ends firmly with raffia and trim.*

2 *A raffia plait can be sewn to form a circular base for a dried-flower wreath as below, or used as a base for a garland or swag.*

Making a moss-covered sphere

Moss-covered spheres are most commonly used for hanging arrangements, but they can provide the base *for a mop-headed, dried-flower tree (see opposite) or for a little bridesmaid's sphere of dried flowers which can be simply carried on a looped ribbon.*

1 *Cut a length of 30cm (1ft) wide chicken wire, a little longer than the planned circumference of the ball. Make a mound of foam pieces on the wire; the foam will be dry if you are making a dried-flower arrangement, and wet if you are arranging fresh flowers. Hold the foam pieces in place with one hand and lift an edge of the wire with the other.*

2 *Holding the first wire edge firmly in place, lift and fold in the remaining edges gently, adding or subtracting pieces of foam to fill out the sphere shape as becomes necessary. Then mould the chicken wire and foam to improve the shape, removing uneven or flat areas where appropriate, and turn sharp wire ends inwards.*

3 *Knot the end of a reel of wire (see p. 179) to the mesh, leaving an end long enough for finishing off. Apply patches of moss (dry for dried-flower arrangements, damp for fresh) and hold them in place, binding the wire around the sphere to secure them. If you use dark-coloured wire, it will not show against the moss, so use plenty.*

4 *When you begin your arrangement, you will be pushing stems and wires through the moss into the foam so it is important to make the covering very firm. Once the whole sphere is covered with moss, bring the binding wire back to the long end of the starting knot and tie off, trimming the ends and concealing them within the moss.*

Making a tree base

Cone-shaped and mop-headed trees are both popular geometrical designs, but you may prefer to make

nature your guide when selecting a shape. The trunk must be firm and the base weighty, so the trunk is set in plaster-of-Paris in an inner pot.

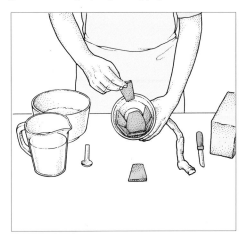

1 *Line a small clay pot with slivers of dry foam. Plaster-of-Paris expands as it sets, and the pieces of foam will allow room for expansion and prevent the pot from cracking. Mix plaster-of-Paris powder to a thick, creamy consistency with water. Two-thirds fill the pot with the mixture, making sure that the dry foam slivers stay in place.*

2 *Place the trunk quickly in the plaster – you will feel it reach the base. Wobble it to ensure that the plaster adheres all round. Supporting the trunk with one hand, turn the pot slowly to see that it looks right from every angle, and then spoon in more plaster to fill the pot to within 12mm (½in) of the rim. Support the trunk until it stands by itself.*

3 *Keep some water handy to pour into the plaster-of-Paris mixing bowl as soon as you have scooped out as much as you need. This will prevent it from setting and cracking the bowl. You can now begin making the head of the tree. Impale your chosen foam base-shape firmly on the trunk. Foam cones and spheres are obtainable from florists but you can sculpt your own from a dry foam "brick". Alternatively, the moss-covered sphere described on p. 186 would serve as a base for a mop-headed tree. Make staples by bending short, thin-gauge stub wires double, and use them to pin dry sphagnum moss to the cone.*

Hanging loops

All hanging flower arrangements (such as wreaths, hanging bunches, spheres and swags) need to have a loop of some sort attached to them so that they can be held in position. The loop you choose should complement your work so that, even from the back, the design is carefully considered. There is only one golden rule: use materials strong enough to support the hanging arrangement over a long period. These examples use raffia and wire. The plaited raffia technique is stronger than the sewn method; the wire loop, securely fixed, is even stronger.

Making a raffia plaited loop

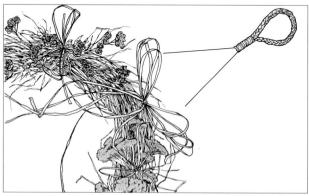

Following the instructions on p. 185, make a raffia plait to the required thickness and length. Form a loop with the plait and bind the cross-over tightly using a stub wire, leaving ends that can be attached to a base. To make a lightweight loop, take several strands of raffia, and enclose them in the looped end of a stub wire before twisting the "eye" shut. Using the stub wire like a needle, push it through the base. Repeat in the opposite direction to form a loop. Cut the wire free and tie off the raffia.

Making a wire loop

1

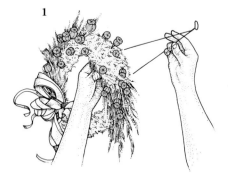

2

3

1 *Cover a stub wire with gutta-percha tape (see p. 179), twist a circle in its middle, and push both ends into the back of the base.*

2 *Pull the two ends back under the base and then push each end into the moss, one on either side of the loop, to secure.*

3 *The wire loop appears in the middle of the back of the base with its wire ends tucked in neatly and securely.*

Wiring plant material

Wiring fresh plant material is usually only necessary when an arrangement requires the flowers and foliage to be contorted into very precise positions, as with wedding posies, circlets, pew ends and complicated garlands. In contrast, dried flowers and foliage often need to be wired to compensate for either the shortness or the fragility of their stems.

Choose a suitable stub wire (see p. 179) – one that will give adequate flexibility and strength as well as the length of stem required. Gutta-percha tape (see p. 179) is used to disguise the unsightly wire.

Lengthening or strengthening stems

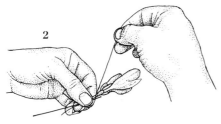

1 *Cut the flower leaving 2.5cm (1in) of stem. Place a stub wire against the stem and a fine rose wire against this so that the longer portion of rose wire protrudes upwards.*

2 *Bend the longer end down and begin to spiral it tightly around the stem, lower end of the rose wire and stub wire.*

3 *Continue winding the rose wire downwards for 7.5cm (3in) to hold the stem firmly in place. Cut the rose wire and fold the end in neatly.*

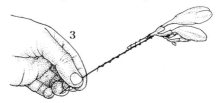

> **SUITABLE PLANTS**
> *Flowers with thin stems, such as fresh freesia*

Wiring a lily-of-the-valley

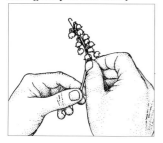

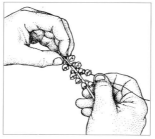

1 *Make a 5mm (⅛in) U shape with the end of a fine rose wire. Hook it near the top of the flower stem, so that the remainder of the wire runs down parallel to the spire of flowers.*

2 *Very gently begin twisting the rose wire round the stem between each single flower, being careful not to break the stem. Continue winding the rose wire down the stem until it is below the lowest flower.*

3 *Wire the remainder of the stem as shown in the previous method.*

> **OTHER SUITABLE PLANTS**
> *Small trails of fresh ivy leaves*

Wiring flower-heads: method 1

Choose a stub wire of the right gauge to support the flower-head firmly. Cut the flower, leaving 2.5cm (1in) of stem. Push the stub wire up the stem and into the base of the flower.

> **SUITABLE PLANTS**
> *Rose, carnation, spray carnation, small lily, orchid*

Wiring flower-heads: method 2

Proceed as for method 1. Push the wire through the flower-head. Bend the wire into a small U shape and pull it downwards, drawing the U-shaped end through the flower. Squeeze the wire ends together.

> **SUITABLE PLANTS**
> *Single chrysanthemum or rose, helichrysum*

Wiring hollow or broken stems

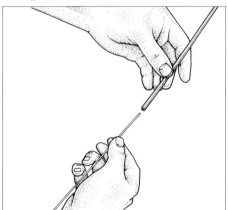

Carefully insert a piece of stub wire of appropriate length and gauge to fit inside the entire stem. Hollow stems can be extended or mended using similar methods; cover the work with gutta-percha tape.

> **SUITABLE PLANTS**
> *Delphinium, hyacinth, larkspur, ranunculus*

Wiring bunches

Holding the bunch in one hand, place a medium-gauge stub wire on top of the stems, its lower end level with their ends. Use the thumb to secure it. Taking the free end of the wire in the other hand, bend it behind the stems at a point 5cm (2in) up from the stem ends. Continue winding it down round the short end and the stems. Use the remaining wire to form an extension of the stems, if required.

Wiring cones

1 *Use heavy-gauge stub wire to form a stem for a cone. Push one end of the wire horizontally through the lowest band of scales so 5cm (2in) juts out on the other side. Wind that end of the wire tightly back round the cone. Twist the wire ends together so that the cone is held firmly.*

2 *Bend the twisted ends under the cone so that the long wire forms a stem from the centre of the base of the cone. Trim the shorter end neatly and conceal the whole length of the wire with gutta-percha tape as described below.*

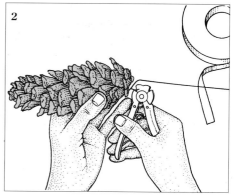

Covering wired stems

1 *Holding the wired flower-head downwards, place a piece of gutta-percha tape the same length as the stub-wire stem, at an angle against the top of the stem.*

2 *Holding the gutta-percha tape so it is stretched taut, revolve the wired stem so that the tape covers itself in a spiral up the wire. Twist to seal the tape at the lower end of the wire.*

Conditioning fresh plant material

Having prepared the container or base and collected the plant material, it is well worth pausing to prepare the material before you make your arrangement. With a little attention at this stage the flowers will last longer and look more attractive.

Even if you have only just cut the stems from the plant, you should always cut them anew at a sharp, diagonal angle to expose a wider surface area. Next, strip all the lower leaves from the stems, otherwise they will simply rot in the water. Remove thorns too. Milky stems should be singed to prevent them from oozing in the vase. And the uppermost buds (which will never flower) of particularly buddy plants should be removed. Scraping the bottom of the sturdier herbaceous stems and slitting *and* scraping the bottom of woody stems helps them to take up water.

Some plant material seems to benefit enormously from the so-called "boiling-water treatment". Although it may seem a drastic measure, the technique forces air downwards out of the stems as the hot water rises upwards, so eliminating airlocks which prevent water from reaching flower-heads and the tips of foliage. Without this treatment, some young plant material can wilt badly, and it can also solve the problem of drooping rose heads.

Finally, stand all plant material in deep water a few hours before arranging, pouring water into hollow stems first.

Preparing stems for arrangement

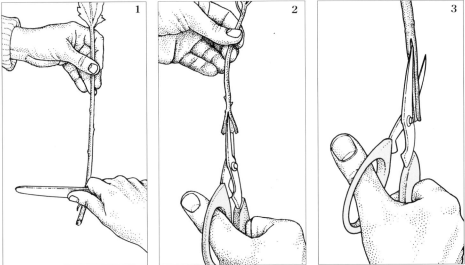

1 Scraping
With a sharp knife or florist's scissors, scrape the bark from the last 5cm (2in) of the stem to encourage it to take up water more quickly and efficiently.

2 Slitting
With a pair of florist's scissors, very carefully cut upwards from the base of the stem, making a cut approximately 5cm (2in) long.

3 Recutting
With florist's scissors, cut the slit stem diagonally to expose a greater surface area to the water.

SUITABLE PLANTS
For scraping, slitting and recutting: woody stems such as azalea, camellia, ceanothus, eucalyptus
For slitting and recutting: robust herbaceous stems

Filling hollow stems: method 1

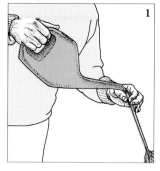

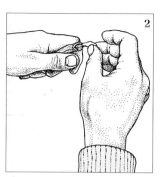

1 *To ensure that water reaches the flower-head quickly, making it last longer, hold the stem upside-down and carefully pour in water.*

2 *When the stem is full, plug the end with a small piece of wet cotton wool and place the stem in a vase of water immediately.*

Filling hollow stems: method 2

1 *Pour water into the stem as above, and then place your thumb tightly over the end.*

2 *Upend the stem into a vase filled with water, preferably the one you will be using, keeping your thumb over the end until it is immersed.*

SUITABLE PLANTS FOR EITHER METHOD
Amaryllis, cow parsley, delphinium, hippeastrum, larkspur, lupin

Treating buddy stems

Singeing milky stems

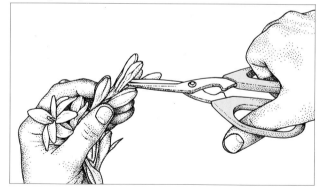

To allow the buds lower down a long and very buddy stem the opportunity to drink some water and therefore increase their chances of eventually flowering, remove the topmost buds (which are extremely unlikely ever to flower) with a pair of florist's scissors. If you take time and care it is not that difficult to trim in such a way that the cut will not be seen by any but the very closest observer.

SUITABLE PLANTS
Gladiolus, kaffir lily, tuberose

To seal an oozing stem, singe the cut end with a lighted match. This will prevent unsightly discoloration of the water and extend the life of the material.

SUITABLE PLANTS
Euphorbia, fern, poppy

Boiling-water treatment

1 *Pour about 5cm (2in) of water into a pan and bring the water to the boil. While waiting for the water to boil, half fill a bucket with tepid water. Having removed the pan to a stable worktop, hold the plant material diagonally and place the ends of the stems in the boiling water for 20 seconds. The stems are held diagonally to prevent the steam affecting the flowers and leaves. Protect short-stemmed flowers with a plastic bag secured with an elastic band.*

2 *Remove the material from the boiling water and immediately plunge the stems into the bucket of tepid water. Leave them to stand in this deep water for several hours before beginning your arrangement so that flowers and foliage can take a good, long drink.*

SUITABLE PLANTS
Alexanders, angelica, bamboo, bear's breeches, bistort, black-eyed Susan, butterfly bush, cock's comb, cow parsley, dogwood, gerbera, globe flower, hollyhock, laburnum, magnolia, mallow, sunflower, viper's bugloss, wormwood

Reviving foliage

Most foliage and some flowers can be refreshed or revived before beginning your arrangement either by totally submerging them in a suitably-sized container filled with cool water or by holding them under a tap and allowing running water to pour very gently all over them. In some instances, when dealing with particularly large pieces of foliage for large-scale arrangements, a bath may be the only available option.

Straightening bendy stems

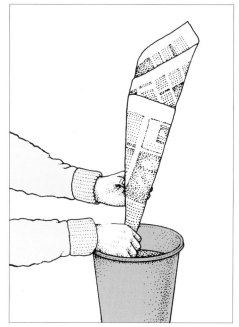

1 *To make bendy-stemmed flowers easier to arrange, cut them on the diagonal, and then wrap them in newspaper in bunches of four or five.*

2 *Secure each newspaper bunch with sticky tape and place in a bucket of water. Leave overnight in a cool place and then use in an arrangement.*

SUITABLE PLANTS
Euphorbia, gerbera, poppy, rose, tulip

Looking after arrangements

Cut flowers do not take a lot of looking after if they have been prepared appropriately. However, there are some basic guidelines that will ensure your arrangements last longer. For instance, it is important not to place fresh flowers directly in front of a radiator, or in strong direct sunlight, as the heat will cause the flowers to droop remarkably quickly. Adding a solution of bleach and sugar to the water in the container will prolong the life of the plant material, and changing the water regularly helps to keep it fresh-smelling. Removing flower-heads as they die keeps the arrangements looking attractive for longer.

Air drying plant material

Air drying is the easiest and most effective method of preserving plant material and most of the plants used in the dried-flower arrangements in this book have been air dried. Depending on the type of plant, the material can be dried hanging upside-down, standing upright in a container, or simply lying on the floor.

Ideally, plant material should be air dried in a room that is cool, dry, well-ventilated and dark, although you can air dry flowers in warmer temperatures and in a room or cupboard without a moving air current. However, it is imperative that the drying room is both dry and dark. If it is not dry, the plant material will rot, especially where the stems or flowers are touching, such as at the tying point of a hanging bunch. If the room is not dark, the flowers will fade extremely quickly.

Harvesting for air drying
All plant material should be picked in dry weather, preferably around or after midday, when any dew will have evaporated. Flowers should be picked approximately four days before they reach their prime. In other words, for the best possible effect a rose should always be picked when the bud is colourful and just as it is on the very point of opening.

Hang drying
Hanging material to dry is the most common method of air drying. Remove all the lower leaves, wipe away any moisture on the stems and then tie the stems together into bunches with lengths of raffia or string, or even an elastic band. Make sure the stems beneath the tie are short enough to be able to hang the bunches upside-down in position. Fan out the flowers, seed-heads and leaves in each bunch so that there is as little contact between the leaves and petals as possible. Then attach the bunches or single stems upside-down to a rail, wire or length of string in your drying place.

Drying upright or flat
Some material air dries well when placed upright in a container, either standing in a small amount of water that slowly evaporates, or simply in an empty vase. As with hanging bunches, the material needs to stand in a cool, dry, well-ventilated, dark place for best results.

Most deciduous and many evergreen leaves are better dried flat, although the leaves will develop crinkly edges. Moss and fir cones can be laid in an airy box or basket to dry and you can sit larger heads of plants such as artichokes on a chicken-wire shelf.

Bunching fresh-cut stems

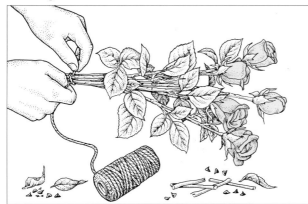

Remove the lower leaves and any thorns to leave bare stems. Assemble a bunch of about five flowers, staggering the positions of the flower-heads. Tie the stems loosely together with string or raffia. Spread out the flowers so that the heads and leaves are well separated and the air can circulate freely around them as they dry.

Spraying grasses and rushes

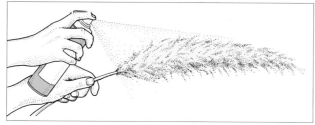

The seed heads of some grasses, especially pampas grass and bulrushes, break up during drying if their surface is not sealed. Spray liberally (out of doors, if possible) with ozone-friendly hair lacquer or another fixative to prevent them from disintegrating.

Hanging to dry

Hanging bunches of plant stems upside-down to dry is one of the simplest methods of air drying. Set up a series of poles or wires about 25cm (10in) apart and at least 15cm (8in) below the ceiling to ensure good air circulation. Either hook the bunches over the poles or attach them to the support with string or raffia ties.

Bunching wired stems

Flowers wired when fresh are very easy to hang dry. Bunch about ten flower-heads together and bind with an elastic band. Gently bend the stem wires so that none of the flower-heads touch. Hang upside-down to dry.

Drying on a pole
This is the quickest way to air dry climbers such as hops and clematis which have attractive seed-heads. Cut them while they are still sappy and twine them round a suspended bamboo pole.

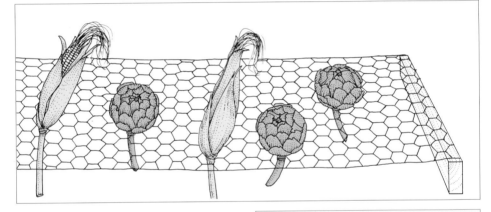

Drying heavy flower- and seed-heads
Secure chicken wire horizontally and high enough to allow long stems to hang freely. Slot each stem through the mesh. Leave the husks of sweet corn in place during drying.

SUITABLE PLANTS
Carline thistle, globe artichoke, lotus, onion, protea, sweet corn

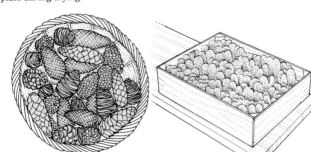

Cones
Leave cones at room temperature for a few days until no moisture is apparent between the scales.

Moss and lichen
Lay in a single layer on a bed of crumpled newspaper. Do not pack tightly.

Drying upright in a container

There are two methods of air drying plant material upright. Some plants dry well when left standing in an empty vase (left). Others dry better when stood in about 5cm (2in) of water. The stems absorb some of the water, which gradually evaporates, leaving the plant material to dry out completely.

SUITABLE PLANTS
With water: gypsophila, hybrid delphinium, hydrangea, lachenalia, mimosa
Without water: bulrush, chenopodium, onion, pampas, sea lavender

Drying flat

Lay the material on an absorbent surface: cardboard or newspaper is ideal. Space the plant material out carefully so that air can circulate around the stems and leaves. Leaves shrivel when dried in this way but keep their colour and retain their natural shape on the stem, which is not the case if they are dried upright or hanging.

SUITABLE PLANTS
Bamboo, all grasses, lavender

Using desiccants

Most plant material can be dried effectively using desiccants, or drying agents, such as silica gel, borax, alum or fine sand. Desiccants draw the moisture out of plant material while leaving it otherwise relatively unchanged, so material dried by this method most closely resembles its fresh counterpart in colour, size and texture. However, there are drawbacks to using desiccants. Silica gel, which dries material the quickest, is very expensive (although crystals can be dried in the oven and re-used), and all desiccants are fiddly to place around the material that you are drying. Also, since they tend to make plant material rather brittle, it is a good idea to wire flower-heads and leaves before drying them (see p. 189).

Silica gel
Silica gel is available as white crystals, or as colour-indicator crystals, which are blue when dry but turn pink as they absorb moisture. They must be ground down in a pestle and mortar or coffee grinder (wash thoroughly afterwards) to at least half their size to envelope material efficiently.

Using silica gel

You will need an airtight tin or box large enough to hold the material you wish to dry. Place a layer of dry crystals in the container and lay the material on top. Pile the crystals round it, using a fine brush to make sure that every part is surrounded by desiccant. Place the lid on the container and seal it with tape. Check the material after two days: it should be firm, and the crystals should be pink. Remove the material from the container as soon as it is dry, otherwise it will become brittle.

Borax, alum and silver sand
Borax and alum should be mixed with fine silver sand before use as desiccants: three parts chemical to two parts sand. Material placed in either will take about ten days to dry; plant material dried in silver sand alone will take about three weeks.

SUITABLE PLANTS
Anemone, camellia, dahlia (small varieties), delphinium, freesia, gentian, gerbera, hellebore, larkspur, lily, narcissus, paeony, ranunculus, rose, zinnia.

1 *A biscuit tin is an ideal container for drying using silica gel. Cover the base of the tin with crystals, and place plant material on top. Remember that heavy stems do not survive this method so replace with wire (see p. 190) before using desiccant.*

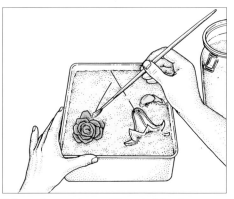

2 *Spoon the crystals round the material and use a fine brush to ease them between petals. Seal the tin and leave for 48 hours. When drying wired material, make sure the container is large enough to accommodate the "stems".*

Preserving with glycerine

This technique depends on replacing the plant's water with glycerine to keep the plant in a stable condition over a long period. Although a few flowers can be preserved in this way, for the most part foliage is better suited to the treatment. Its advantage is that the plant material remains supple, and therefore tends to look more natural; its disadvantage is that it causes dramatic colour changes, plant material usually becoming dark brown or khaki.

For strong-stemmed material, make a solution of 40 per cent glycerine to 60 per cent hot water. Stand the stems in about 10cm (4in) solution, making sure that the container supports the stems. Leave in a cool, dark place for at least six days. Terminate the process when beads of glycerine start to form on the upper parts of the plant material. Remove from the solution and wash thoroughly.

To treat individual leaves in this way, make a stronger solution of 50 per cent glycerine to 50 per cent water. Leaves will absorb the glycerine they need in about six days.

SUITABLE PLANTS
Stemmed material: copper beech, elaeagnus, hydrangea, laurel, moluccella
Leaves: aspidistra, choisya, eucalyptus, holly, magnolia, mahonia, pin oak

---

Preserving strong-stemmed material

1 *Remove leaves and branches from the lower stems. Slit woody stem ends upwards for 5cm (2in). Finally, cut the stems at a sharp, diagonal angle.*

2 *Stand in the solution, making sure that hollow stems are supported by wire (see p. 190) and leave in a cool, dark place for 6–10 days.*

Preserving foliage

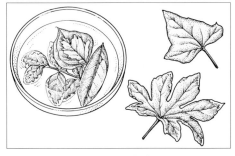

1 *Immerse single leaves or sprigs in solution, and leave in a dark place.*

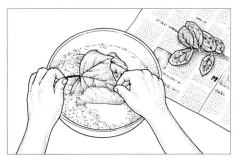

2 *When the leaves have darkened, remove and wash in soapy water. Pat dry.*

Colouring dried or preserved material

Many festive arrangements benefit from the inclusion of some brightly coloured dried-plant material, and you can enliven much tired-looking material quite enormously by colouring it. There are several methods of colouring plant material.

Material preserved in glycerine

If you add dye to a glycerine solution (see p. 201), the plant material will drink the dye at the same time as the solution. Since foliage often turns a rather muddy colour once it has absorbed glycerine, this is a good way to alter its drab appearance. Green dye, for example, will result in leaves that are darker than fresh ones, but they will certainly be more attractive than undyed ones.

You can also add artificial colours to foliage in this way. Red dye will give leaves such as eucalyptus an autumnal glow, while rust dye adds a warm, mellow look to lime bracts and copper beech leaves.

Alternatively, adding bleach to the glycerine solution will leave the plant material a creamy colour.

Dyeing material as it air dries

If you are standing material in water before letting it air dry, you could add some dye to the water. The material will then drink the dye with the water before it starts to dry. For most purposes, it is best that the plant material should look absolutely natural when dried, so try to dye it a colour that actually exists in a variety of the plant that you are dyeing. In general, blue is the least satisfactory colour often producing extremely unnatural-looking plants.

Colour spraying and painting

Special spray paints for colouring both fresh and dried flowers are available in a huge range of colours. Some are particularly useful. Sea lavender, which dries to a grey-white, can be sprayed a natural-looking pale yellow or pink. A combination of the two will result in an attractive peach colour.

Brighter colour sprays or fast-drying paint are ideal for festive decorations where you want to create a splash of colour. Poppy seed-heads and love-in-a-mist seed-heads look wonderful coloured bright red, bright pink or rich green. Fir cones, nuts and the delicate umbels of lovage, cow parsley, coriander and fennel look great sprayed silver or gold and then dredged with glitter before the paint has dried, so that the sparkling crystals adhere well. However, for all-year-round arrangements it is best to use only colours that are less striking and more natural-looking.

Colour spraying

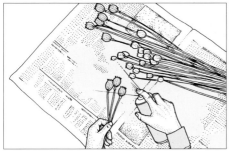

Taking three or four stems at a time, spray poppy seed-heads thoroughly with red paint for a cheerfully festive effect at any time of the year.

Glittering

Spray fir cones with silver paint. Then sprinkle glitter over them for extra sparkle to make an attractive table centrepiece or tree decoration for Christmas.

Storing dried and preserved material

If you are harvesting and drying or pressing your own material you will probably have periods of surplus. When you need to store material for many months, you must be careful about how you pack it.

Any flowers that are hanging in bunches from the ceiling to dry can simply be left hanging after they have dried, so long as they are hanging out of direct sunlight. Similarly, any material that you are drying in a cupboard can be left where it is.

The most usual method of storing dried plant material, however, is to pack it away in sealed cardboard boxes, which are then placed in a cool, dry place, preferably with some ventilation. Before packing dried material ensure that it is completely dry. If there is still some moisture in just one flower, rot will soon set in once the box is packed. The cardboard boxes used for taking fresh flowers to market are probably the most suitable.

Air-dried plant material needs to be held firmly in place so that no pressure is placed on flower-heads, leaves or seed-heads. Layers of pleated tissue paper or newspaper can be used to ensure that each bunch is well protected from its neighbour. Very strong material, such as cones or artichoke heads, requires no special protection and is best laid in a box or basket and stored in a cool, dry place until required.

Glycerined material should be packed in the same way as air-dried material. However, on no account pack glycerined and air-dried material in the same box, as plant material that has been preserved with glycerine still retains a certain amount of moisture and will therefore spoil dried flowers and foliage immediately.

You can also store pressed material in much the same way. Place it in a box, layering it between sheets of blotting paper, newspaper or tissue paper.

Packing dried-flower bundles
Glycerine- and air-dried material can be packed in the same way, although on no account mix the two. Plant material has to be held in place so that no pressure is placed on flower-heads, leaves or seed-heads. Wrap fragile bunches in tissue paper first, and then pack them so that the stalks of the plants on one layer are separated from the heads of the material on the next layer with strips of pleated tissue or soft newspaper.

Wrapping delicate bunches

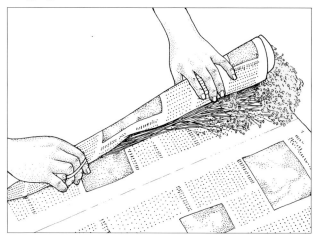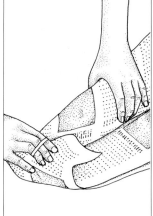

1 *When storing bunches of delicate-headed flowers, such as roses, wrap each bunch carefully in newspaper or tissue paper before packing it in a box. This will help to reduce pressure from neighbouring*

material. Roll a sheet of newspaper loosely around the bunch to form a cone shape. It is best to begin by folding the edge of the paper inwards once to make the cone of flowers more secure.

2 *Tuck in the narrow end of the cone as you roll the newspaper and, when you have wrapped the bunch, secure it with sticky tape or a small elastic band, making sure you put no pressure on the stems.*

Wrapping individual hydrangeas

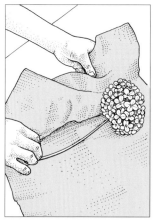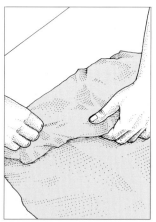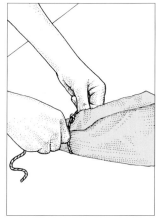

1 *Both types of hydrangea heads – mop-head and lace-cap – are particularly fragile once they have been dried, and it is important that they should be individually wrapped so that the petals are not damaged before being stored, hanging singly. Begin by placing each flower-head on a large sheet of tissue paper.*

2 *Gently form the tissue paper into a loose cone around the stem and flower, taking great care not to crush the delicate flower head as you wrap it. Once the tissue paper is in position, secure it carefully but firmly, using a small piece of adhesive tape. Move the flower head as little as possible while you are wrapping and securing it.*

3 *Take a long piece of string or raffia and tie the cone about 10cm (4in) from the bottom. Form a hanging loop with the remainder of the string or raffia and hang the flower-heads individually in a cool, dry, well-ventilated place until required. Your work will quickly be ruined if left in a damp atmosphere to store.*

Wrapping large seed-heads

1 *To protect a delicate seed-head on a strong stem, pleat a strip of tissue paper 18–20cm (7–8in) wide and 60cm (2ft) long.*

2 *Hold the pleated tissue 5cm (2in) below the seed-head and fan out the pleats carefully to form a ruff around the head.*

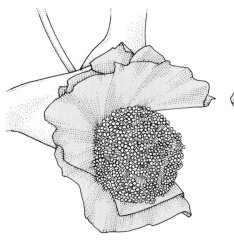

3 *Secure the tissue-paper wrapping in position by making a string or raffia tie just below the point where the protective paper ruff fans out at the top of the stem.*

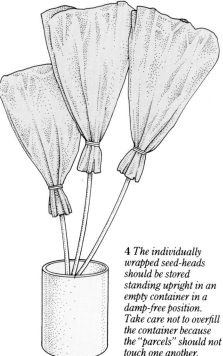

4 *The individually wrapped seed-heads should be stored standing upright in an empty container in a damp-free position. Take care not to overfill the container because the "parcels" should not touch one another.*

SUITABLE PLANTS
Bulrush, giant hogweed, onion, tall grasses such as pampas grass

· CHAPTER NINE ·

DIRECTORY OF FLOWERS AND FOLIAGE

There is an almost bewildering wealth of plant material for the flower arranger to choose from. Of course, some plants are unsuitable for arranging, maybe because of their size or possibly their prickly spines, and some will not dry well. The following pages set out a wide selection of the plants that can be used successfully. Each entry gives a brief description of the plant, the time of year when it is at its best, plus brief advice on how to prepare it for arranging. Additional details on the conditioning of fresh plant material appears on pages 192–5 and on drying and preserving material on pages 196–201.

Traditional herbaceous border
Clumps of lofty delphiniums claim the attention with a supporting cast of Alchemilla mollis, *with its clouds of tiny, soft lime-green flowers, and pale pink shrub and climbing roses. Altogether sharper notes are struck by the small crimson shrub rose and the orangey bracts just making an appearance on the* Euphorbia griffithii. *A low, relatively wide, well-established box hedge makes a wonderfully trim border in delightful contrast with the rampageous climbers on the wall behind.*

Acacia Mimosa, wattle

Trees with clusters of fragrant yellow flowers and grey-green, finely cut leaves. The flowering branches of mimosa air dry well, retaining excellent flower colour.
AVAILABILITY Spring.
CONDITIONING (FRESH) Scrape, slit and recut stems and then stand in deep water and cover with plastic bag for a day.
PICKING FOR DRYING Spring.
DRYING METHODS Air dry by hanging.

Acanthus Bear's breeches

Herbaceous plants with tall spikes of mauve, purple/white hooded flowers, with large, handsome glossy leaves. Long lasting in water.
AVAILABILITY Late summer.
CONDITIONING (FRESH) Slit and recut stems. Follow with boiling-water treatment and stand in deep water for three to four hours.
PICKING FOR DRYING Autumn.
DRYING METHODS Air dry flowers by hanging.

Acer Maple

Trees with green, yellow, brown and purple foliage, plus good autumn tints. Some maples are very slow growing and therefore unsuitable for repeated cutting. Some have good foliage and fragrant flowers in spring.
AVAILABILITY Summer for natural leaf colours; autumn for tints.
CONDITIONING (FRESH) Scrape, slit and recut stems and then stand in deep water for several hours. Float or submerge individual leaves for small arrangements.
PICKING FOR DRYING Summer and autumn.
DRYING METHODS Dry both summer and autumn foliage between newspaper in box. Press individual leaves in flower press.

Achillea Yarrow

Flat-headed, yellow flowers over a feathery foliage. Also pink/red and white varieties. *A. ptarmic* has white button-like flowers. All long lasting.
AVAILABILITY Summer, autumn.
CONDITIONING (FRESH) Slit and recut stems and then stand in deep water for several hours.
PICKING FOR DRYING Summer.
DRYING METHODS Air dry by hanging or by standing in container without water.

Acidanthera

White gladiolus-type flowers with dark blotches in the throat. Sweetly scented. Tall with thin, long leaves.
AVAILABILITY Early autumn.
CONDITIONING (FRESH) Stand in deep water for several hours.
PICKING FOR DRYING Early autumn.
DRYING METHODS Dry individual flowers in desiccant.

Aconitum Monkshood

Tall spikes of deep blue, hooded flowers. Also lighter blue, white and cream varieties. Poisonous.
AVAILABILITY Summer, autumn.
CONDITIONING (FRESH) Boiling-water treatment or plug stem and then stand in deep water for several hours.
PICKING FOR DRYING Summer.
DRYING METHODS Air dry by hanging.

Aesculus Horse chestnut

Trees with "sticky buds" opening in water to reveal young leaves. Brown, shiny fruit, commonly known as "conkers". The huge leaves look good with clusters of the maturing fruit in large arrangements. Not suitable for drying.
AVAILABILITY Buds in spring; fruit in autumn.
CONDITIONING (FRESH) Scrape, slit and recut stems and then stand in deep water for several hours.

Agapanthus African lily

Round globes of blue flowers in various shades. Also white varieties. Strap-like leaves. Last quite well in water. Not suitable for drying.
AVAILABILITY Late summer to autumn.
CONDITIONING (FRESH) Stand in deep water for several hours.

Ajuga Bugle

Short ground-covering plants with spikes of blue flowers. There are varieties with pink flowers and also some with variegated or coloured leaves. Medium lasting. Pretty in miniature arrangements. Not suitable for drying.
AVAILABILITY Spring and summer.
CONDITIONING (FRESH) Stand in deep water for several hours.

Alchemilla Lady's mantle

Feathery sprays of small, green-yellow flowers. Soft, round leaves holding pearls of water. Long lasting.
AVAILABILITY Spring to early autumn.
CONDITIONING (FRESH) Stand in deep water for several hours.
PICKING FOR DRYING Early summer.
DRYING METHODS Air dry by hanging. Mature flowers: preserve by standing in glycerine.

Allium Decorative onion

Bulbs producing round globes of purple or pink flowers. Also blue, white and yellow varieties. Long lasting. Dried, they can be used for their flower- or seed-heads.
AVAILABILITY Spring and summer.
CONDITIONING (FRESH) Stand in deep water for several hours.
PICKING FOR DRYING Summer.
DRYING METHODS Air dry by hanging or standing in container without water or preserve seed-heads by standing in glycerine.

Alstroemeria Peruvian lily

Trumpets of pink, red, orange, yellow and white flowers on longish stems. Good seed pods. Medium lasting.

AVAILABILITY Summer. All year from florists.

CONDITIONING (FRESH) Stand in deep water for several hours.

PICKING FOR DRYING Summer.

DRYING METHODS Air dry seed-heads by hanging. Dry individual flowers with desiccant.

Althaea Hollyhock

Old-fashioned flowers with very tall spikes of red, pink, purple, yellow or white. They grow in any conditions and have excellent seed-heads.

AVAILABILITY Summer.

CONDITIONING (FRESH) Boiling-water treatment for stems and then stand in deep water for several hours before using.

PICKING FOR DRYING Summer.

DRYING METHODS Air dry seed-heads by hanging. Dry individual flowers with desiccant.

Amaranthus Love-lies-bleeding

Half-hardy annual plants with long ropes of crimson flowers. Also green variety available. Long lasting.

AVAILABILITY Summer, autumn.

CONDITIONING (FRESH) Remove most of the leaves and stand in deep water for several hours.

PICKING FOR DRYING Summer.

DRYING METHODS Air dry by hanging or standing in container without water or preserve by standing in glycerine. If dried hanging up, the tassel of the flowers dries straight. For a trailing effect, they should be dried upright.

Amaryllis Belladonna lily

Bulbs with fragrant pink or white flowers on long stems, which can also be used as pot plants.

AVAILABILITY Autumn in gardens. Winter and spring from florists.

CONDITIONING (FRESH) Stand in deep water for several hours.

PICKING FOR DRYING Autumn.

DRYING METHODS Dry individual flowers with desiccant.

See also *Hippeastrum.*

Ammobium Winged everlasting, sandflower

These simple little white daisy flowers retain a good white when dried. They have thin stems near the flower-heads so wire bunches if you want them to stand upright, otherwise allow them to cascade on their own stems.

AVAILABILITY Summer.

CONDITIONING (FRESH) Stand in deep water for several hours.

PICKING FOR DRYING Summer.

DRYING METHODS Air dry by hanging.

Anaphalis Pearl everlasting

Silver-grey foliage plants that have small and white, yellow-centred flowers.

AVAILABILITY Summer, autumn.

CONDITIONING (FRESH) Stand in deep water for several hours before using.

PICKING FOR DRYING Summer before fully open.

DRYING METHODS Air dry by hanging or standing in container without water.

Anemone Windflower

There are several distinct anemones. First there are the spring-flowering types: wood anemones which are short and delicate in shades of white, pink and blue; and the De Caen types, which are bright and in brash shades of red, blue and mauve. The autumn-flowering Japanese anemones are much taller and robust. These are white or pink.

AVAILABILITY Spring or autumn. De Caen are available from florists for most of the year.

CONDITIONING (FRESH) Stand in deep water for several hours.

PICKING FOR DRYING Spring and summer.

DRYING METHODS Press in flower press or dry individual flower-heads with desiccant.

Anethum Dill

The white flower-heads form a delicate tracery in arrangements. Stems retain their aromatic scent for a considerable time.

AVAILABILITY Summer.

CONDITIONING (FRESH) Boiling-water treatment and then stand in deep water for several hours.

PICKING FOR DRYING Summer.

DRYING METHODS Air dry by hanging.

Angelica

Large, white-green domes of flowers and bold foliage, usually found in herb gardens. Tall. Both flowers and seed-heads good in arrangements.

AVAILABILITY Summer.

CONDITIONING (FRESH) Boiling-water treatment for stems and then stand in deep water for several hours.

DRYING METHODS Preserve seed-heads by standing in glycerine.

Anigozanthos Kangaroo paw

Delicate cream trumpet flowers with rust- or yellow-coloured calyx. Not suitable for fresh arrangements.

PICKING FOR DRYING Autumn.

DRYING METHODS Air dry by hanging.

Anthemis Chamomile

The small centre of the white flower dries to a sturdy bobble. Try dying them a bright colour. They are not suitable for fresh arrangements.

PICKING FOR DRYING Summer.

DRYING METHODS Air dry by hanging.

Anthriscus Cow parsley, Queen Anne's lace

Tall, wild plants of the hedge-rows with large, flat heads of white flowers above delicate, lacy foliage. Last well but tend to exude a fine, sticky honeydew.

AVAILABILITY Spring.

CONDITIONING (FRESH) Boiling-water treatment for stems and then stand in deep water for several hours.

DRYING METHODS Air dry seed-heads by hanging.

Anthurium **Painter's palette**

Exotic, greenhouse plants with heart-shaped leaves and a curious cylindrical flower coming from a bright heart-shaped bract. Five hundred species giving a large variety of colour and shape. Very long lasting in water. Not suitable for drying.

AVAILABILITY Summer. All year from florists.

CONDITIONING (FRESH) Stand in deep water for several hours.

Antirrhinum **Snapdragon**

Annual bedding plants. Old-fashioned-looking flowers with a good range of all colours except blue. The modern varieties are the best for arrangements. Short lasting in water. Not suitable for drying.

AVAILABILITY Summer.

CONDITIONING (FRESH) Stand in deep water for several hours.

Aquilegia **Columbine, granny's bonnet**

Old-fashioned cottage flowers. Short-lived in water but good as cut flowers because of the shape and variety of colours. All are suitable for cutting, but McKana hybrids are the best.

AVAILABILITY Summer.

CONDITIONING (FRESH) Stand in deep water for several hours.

PICKING FOR DRYING Summer.

DRYING METHODS Dry individual flowers with desiccant.

Arbutus **Strawberry tree**

Unusual trees in that the white flowers and the previous year's berries appear at the same time. The fruit look like strawberries. Not suitable for drying.

AVAILABILITY Late autumn.

CONDITIONING (FRESH) Scrape, slit and recut stems and then stand in deep water for several hours.

Armeria **Thrift, sea pink**

Cushions of short stems topped by a pink head of flowers. Deep pink and red varieties are avail-

able, but the leaves are of no significance in arrangements. Quite a long life in water.

AVAILABILITY Summer.

CONDITIONING (FRESH) Stand in deep water for several hours.

PICKING FOR DRYING Summer.

DRYING METHODS Air dry by hanging.

Artemisia **Wormwood**

Valuable for their tall stems of silvery-grey foliage. Flowers insignificant except for *A. lactiflora*, which has green leaves and masses of small cream flowers. Long lasting in water.

AVAILABILITY Summer, autumn.

CONDITIONING (FRESH) Slit and recut stems. Follow with boiling-water treatment and then stand in deep water for several hours.

PICKING FOR DRYING Summer.

DRYING METHODS Air dry by hanging.

Arum **Cuckoo-pint, lords-and-ladies**

Native plants useful for their shiny spring foliage. *A. italicum* 'Pictum' is valuable as it has leaves with cream marbling throughout the winter. The spikes of red berries, although useful, are poisonous. Not suitable for drying.

AVAILABILITY Leaves: winter and spring. Berries: autumn.

CONDITIONING (FRESH) Submerge leaves in water for half an hour. Secure stems at top and bottom with elastic bands to prevent splitting and stand in deep water for an hour.

Arundinaria **Bamboo**

Slender stems with grass-like leaves. Rarely flowers. Bamboo dries easily and its leaves turn a bluey-green.

AVAILABILITY All year.

CONDITIONING (FRESH) Two or three minutes in boiling vinegar to prevent leaves curling, then stand in deep water for several hours.

PICKING FOR DRYING Summer.

DRYING METHODS Air dry by standing in a container without water or lying flat, or preserve by standing in glycerine.

Asparagus

Valuable for the spikes or spears when they first appear, or tall fine, feathery foliage later on. In autumn they carry red berries, but the leaves drop readily once they start yellowing.

AVAILABILITY Spears: early summer. Foliage: summer and throughout year from florists.

CONDITIONING (FRESH) Stand in deep water for several hours.

PICKING FOR DRYING Summer.

DRYING METHODS Press foliage in flower press.

Aster **Michaelmas daisy**

A good range of tall, brightly coloured daisies. There are many cultivars available and also more delicate species with airy sprays of small flowers. They last very well in water.

AVAILABILITY Autumn.

CONDITIONING (FRESH) Slit and recut stems and then stand in deep water for several hours.

PICKING FOR DRYING Autumn.

DRYING METHODS Press flowers in flowers press.

See also *Callistephus*.

Astilbe

Tapering plumes of feathery flowers in a range of colours from pink through mauves to red as well as white and cream. Lots of varieties. The leaves are also very decorative. Not long lasting in water. Worth cutting after brown seed-heads have formed.

AVAILABILITY Summer. Seed-heads: Autumn.

CONDITIONING (FRESH) Stand in deep water for several hours.

PICKING FOR DRYING Summer.

DRYING METHODS Air dry by hanging. Press leaves in flower press.

Astrantia **Masterwort**

Curiously shaped greenish-white

flowers, each like a little posy. There are shell pink and red forms, which grow to a medium height with good foliage. Last well in water. Combine well in arrangements with phlox and larkspur.
AVAILABILITY Summer, autumn.
CONDITIONING (FRESH) Stand in deep water for several hours.
PICKING FOR DRYING Summer.
DRYING METHODS Air dry by hanging.

Athyrium Lady fern, female fern
The green graceful fronds of lady fern look beautiful when used as a background to flowers or when featured with other foliage.
AVAILABILITY Summer.
CONDITIONING (FRESH) Boiling-water treatment and then stand in deep water for several hours.
PICKING FOR DRYING Summer.
DRYING METHODS Press, either between newspaper under carpet where there is no traffic or alternatively in a flower press.

Aucuba Spotted laurel
Shrubs that are useful for their all-year-round shiny green foliage. Variegated forms are available. Female plants also carry brilliant red berries. Not suitable for drying.
AVAILABILITY Foliage: all year. Berries: autumn and winter.
CONDITIONING (FRESH) Scrape, slit and recut stems and then stand in deep water for several hours.

Avena Oats
The delicate nodding heads of oats can be dried in their unripened green state or their ripened state, when they will be honey-coloured.
AVAILABILITY Summer.
CONDITIONING (FRESH) Stand in deep water for several hours.
PICKING FOR DRYING Summer.
DRYING METHODS Air dry by hanging or standing in container without water.

Azalea
A type of *Rhododendron* with brightly coloured flowers. They can be used as cut flowers or dwarf varieties can be grown in pots for display. Many cultivars are available; some are particularly fragrant. Do not last long in water.
AVAILABILITY Spring, winter in pots if forced.
CONDITIONING (FRESH) Scrape, slit and recut stems. Follow with boiling-water treatment and then stand in deep water for several hours.
PICKING FOR DRYING Spring.
DRYING METHODS Press individual flowers in flower press.

Ballota
Perennials or sub-shrubs valuable for their furry, circular leaves, which are cupped around the arching stems. The "furriness" gives the leaves a greyish-green appearance. The flowers are insignificant. Last very well in water.
AVAILABILITY Summer, autumn.
CONDITIONING (FRESH) Boiling-water treatment for stems and then stand in deep water, not submerging the leaves.
PICKING FOR DRYING Summer and autumn.
DRYING METHODS Preserve by standing in glycerine (removing leaves after flowering) or air dry by hanging.

Banksia
Australian honeysuckle
Australian evergreen trees and shrubs with dramatic cones of yellow or red flowers. Tender and can only be grown in conservatories or greenhouses except in very mild areas.
AVAILABILITY Summer.
CONDITIONING (FRESH) Scrape, slit and recut stems and then stand in deep water for several hours.
PICKING FOR DRYING Spring.
DRYING METHODS Air dry by hanging.

Berberis Barberry
Spiny shrubs with green or purple foliage and yellow or orange flowers. Red berries are particularly useful in autumn. Not suitable for drying.
AVAILABILITY Foliage: spring to autumn, some species all year. Flowers: spring. Berries: autumn.
CONDITIONING (FRESH) Remove lower thorns. Scrape, slit and recut stems and then stand in deep water for several hours.

Bergenia Elephant ear
Large fleshy-leaved plants with drooping spikes of varying shades of pink flowers. Both leaves and flowers are good for fresh arrangements. Not suitable for drying.
AVAILABILITY Flowers: spring. Leaves: all year.
CONDITIONING (FRESH) Stand in deep water for several hours.

Betula Birch
These trees produce graceful bare branches in winter or sprays of fresh green leaves in spring. They also have small catkins in spring and catkin-like seed in autumn, the latter dropping badly. There are many forms of birch with varying bark colour and leaf size. Colour dried twigs for use in Christmas decorations and arrangements or use to make a wreath base.
AVAILABILITY Branches: all year. Leaves: spring, summer.
CONDITIONING (FRESH) Scrape, slit and recut stems and then stand in deep water for several hours.
PICKING FOR DRYING Winter.
DRYING METHODS Air dry twigs and branches in arrangement.

Bouvardia
Tender greenhouse shrubs with tight heads of tubular flowers in pink, white and yellow. Some species are fragrant. Not suitable for drying.
CONDITIONING (FRESH) Slit and

recut stems, follow with boiling-water treatment and stand in deep water for several hours.

Brassica Cabbage
Many brassicas are very decorative, not only the round leafy varieties, but the tall spires of Brussels sprouts, white and purple buds of the broccolis, the white curds of cauliflowers and the curly leaves of kale. Both cabbages and Brussels have red forms. There are also brightly coloured ornamental cabbages. Not suitable for drying.
AVAILABILITY Cabbages: all year. Brussels: autumn and winter. Ornamentals: autumn.
CONDITIONING (FRESH) Submerge leaves for half an hour then stand in water for another half hour.

Briza Quaking grass
Graceful grasses with drooping compact heads which move in the slightest draught. Pale green when fresh. Quite unlike any other grass in shape. Long lasting and make a good filler in an arrangement.
AVAILABILITY Summer, autumn.
CONDITIONING (FRESH) None.
PICKING FOR DRYING Summer.
DRYING METHODS Air dry by standing in container without water or hanging.

Brodiaea
Bulbous plants similar to the decorative allium. Blue or purple heads on medium stems. Leaves often shrivel before flower opens, so of no consequence.
AVAILABILITY Summer.
CONDITIONING (FRESH) Stand in deep water for several hours.
PICKING FOR DRYING Summer.
DRYING METHODS Press individual flowers in flower press.

Brunnera
These herbaceous plants have myriad pale blue flowers floating above the heart-shaped leaves. Not very tall. Last reasonably well in water.

AVAILABILITY Early summer.
CONDITIONING (FRESH) Slit and recut stems then stand in deep water for several hours.
PICKING FOR DRYING Early summer.
DRYING METHODS Press sprays of flowers in flower press.

Buddleia Butterfly bush
Fragrant shrubs with long spikes of mauve, purple or white flowers. Also species with globes of orange or yellow flowers. The grey-silver or green foliage should be removed as it does not last well. Not suitable for drying.
AVAILABILITY Spring, summer and autumn.
CONDITIONING (FRESH) Boiling-water treatment for stems and then stand in deep water for several hours.

Bupleurum sp. Bupleurum
This tender, semi-evergreen Australian plant makes a good background filler, both for its green foliage and small white flower-heads.
AVAILABILITY Summer, autumn.
CONDITIONING (FRESH) Slit and recut stems and then stand in deep water for several hours.
PICKING FOR DRYING Mid to late summer.
DRYING METHODS Air dry flowers by hanging.

Buxus Box
Evergreen shrubs with small glossy leaves. Last a very long time in water. Also variegated variety available. Flowers of no consequence.
AVAILABILITY All year.
CONDITIONING (FRESH) Scrape, slit and recut stems and then stand in deep water for several hours.
PICKING FOR DRYING All year.
DRYING METHODS Preserve by standing in glycerine.

Caladium Angel wings
Tender pot plants grown for their foliage. The large, heart-shaped

leaves have veins of a contrasting colour. The leaves can be green, white, cream or pale pink. They do not last long if cut. Not suitable for drying.
AVAILABILITY Summer.
CONDITIONING (FRESH) Submerge leaves in water for half an hour before using.

Calendula Pot marigold
Hardy annuals with bright yellow or vibrant orange flowers. Old-fashioned, cottage flowers. They last quite well in water.
AVAILABILITY Summer.
CONDITIONING (FRESH) Stand in deep water for several hours.
PICKING FOR DRYING Summer.
DRYING METHODS Air dry quickly by hanging in a warm cupboard or warming oven. Press individual flowers in flower press.

Callistemon Bottle-brush tree
Half-hardy and tender trees from Australia with beautiful bright red or yellow flowers with spikes of stamens that closely resemble bottle brushes. Bottle-brush provides one of the best reds of any dried flower.
AVAILABILITY Summer.
CONDITIONING (FRESH) Scrape, slit and recut stems and then stand in deep water for several hours.
PICKING FOR DRYING Summer.
DRYING METHODS Air dry flowers by hanging.

Callistephus China aster
Daisy-like annuals available in a wide range of bright colours. Come in singles or doubles. Last well in water.
AVAILABILITY Autumn.
CONDITIONING (FRESH) Stand in deep water for several hours.
PICKING FOR DRYING Late summer and autumn.
DRYING METHODS Press individual flowers in flower press or dry in desiccant.

Camassia Quamash
Bulbs producing long stems with

spikes of large, star-shaped flowers in blue or white. They do not last very long in water but are valuable for their blue colour. Allow seed-heads to dry on plant.
AVAILABILITY Summer.
CONDITIONING (FRESH) Stand in deep water for several hours.
PICKING FOR DRYING Flowers: summer.
DRYING METHODS Dry individual flowers in desiccant.

Camellia
Superb white, pink or red flowers set against glossy green leaves. There are many hardy cultivars to choose from. Long lasting in water.
AVAILABILITY Late winter and spring. Earlier from florists.
CONDITIONING (FRESH) Scrape, slit and recut stems and then stand in deep water for several hours.
PICKING FOR DRYING Flowers: spring. Leaves: summer.
DRYING METHODS Flowers: dry with desiccant or crystallize. Leaves: preserve by standing in glycerine.

Campanula Bellflower
A vast range of blue flowers from very short to tall, the shorter having single bells, the taller whole spikes of flowers. Very cool in appearance. White forms are also available. They last well in water.
AVAILABILITY Summer.
CONDITIONING (FRESH) Stand in deep water for several hours. Last longer if bees excluded from room.
PICKING FOR DRYING Summer.
DRYING METHODS Press individual flowers in flower press.

Capsicum Chillies, sweet pepper
Green or bright red fruit with shiny skins producing good highlights in arrangements. Purchased fruit do not last as long as home-produced. Dried peppers tend to shrivel.

AVAILABILITY Autumn or all year from greengrocers.
CONDITIONING (FRESH) Polish.
PICKING FOR DRYING Autumn.
DRYING METHODS Air dry by hanging.

Carlina Carline thistle
These beautiful, but vicious, large flower thistles, 10–15cm (4–5in) across, are one of the strongest-looking dried flowers and, although they have a wild look about them, they suit both formal and informal arrangements. Their prickles, however, make them unsuitable for fresh arrangements.
PICKING FOR DRYING Autumn.
DRYING METHODS Air dry by standing in container without water.

Carthamus Safflower
Pick just as the orange petals begin to show for best dried results. The flower colour is strong and safflower will show well if arranged in groups. It is worth drying safflower with the upper leaves on the stem, as they provide an excellent foil for the flowers.
AVAILABILITY Summer.
CONDITIONING (FRESH) Stand in deep water for several hours.
PICKING FOR DRYING Summer.
DRYING METHODS Air dry by hanging.

Castanea Sweet chestnut
Good, large-leaved foliage; fluffy yellow flowers (some might not like the smell) and then light green, spiny fruit cases and shiny brown nuts.
AVAILABILITY Leaves: spring and summer. Flowers: summer. Fruit cases and nuts: autumn.
CONDITIONING (FRESH) Scrape, slit and recut stems and then stand in deep water for several hours. Polish nuts.
PICKING FOR DRYING Spring and summer.
DRYING METHODS Preserve leaves standing in glycerine.

Catananche Cupid's dart
Pale blue, dark eyed flowers with a papery calyx on thin stems. Very long lasting in water or as dried flowers.
AVAILABILITY Summer, autumn.
CONDITIONING (FRESH) Stand in deep water for several hours.
PICKING FOR DRYING Summer.
DRYING METHODS Air dry by hanging, press in flower press or dry in desiccant.

Cattleya
A wonderful range of epiphytic orchids with broad lips. The largest flowers can be up to 25cm (10in) across. Many species and cultivars are available giving a good range of colours with purple predominating. Some are fragrant. Short-stemmed and delicate. Not suitable for drying.
AVAILABILITY All year.
CONDITIONING (FRESH) Stand in deep water for several hours.

Ceanothus Californian lilac
Evergreen and deciduous shrubs with fluffy round clusters of varying shades of blue flowers. The evergreen varieties have particularly good foliage. Not suitable for drying.
AVAILABILITY Spring and early summer.
CONDITIONING (FRESH) Scrape, slit and recut stems and then stand in deep water for several hours.

Celosia Cock's comb
Spectacular plants with bright red or yellow feathery plumes.
AVAILABILITY Late summer and autumn.
CONDITIONING (FRESH) Boiling-water treatment for stems and then stand in deep water for several hours.
PICKING FOR DRYING Summer.
DRYING METHODS Air dry by hanging.

Centaurea Cornflower, sweet sultan
Long-lasting annuals. The basic

colour is blue but there is now a good range available including white, pink, mauve and red. The variety sweet sultan (*C. moschata*) is deliciously fragrant.
AVAILABILITY Summer.
CONDITIONING (FRESH) Stand in deep water for several hours.
PICKING FOR DRYING Summer.
DRYING METHODS Air dry by hanging or dry in desiccant.

Centranthus **Valerian**
Large heads of deep pink or red flowers with fleshy stems and foliage. There are also white forms available. None is suitable for drying.
AVAILABILITY Summer.
CONDITIONING (FRESH) Boiling-water treatment for young stems. Stand in deep water for several hours.

Chaenomeles
Ornamental quince
Waxy, apple-blossom type flowers clustered tight to the leafless branches. Mainly shades of red but also white, pink and orange. Curiously coloured, pear-shaped fruit.
AVAILABILITY Flowers: spring. Fruit: autumn.
CONDITIONING (FRESH) Scrape, slit and recut stems and then stand in deep water for several hours.
PICKING FOR DRYING Spring.
DRYING METHODS Press flowers in flower press.

Chaerophyllum **Chervil**
The flowering umbels of chervil and most similar umbelliferous plants, such as fennel, cow parsley and hogweed, can be pressed to form beautiful radiating patterns of stems and flowers. The seed-heads can also be dried successfully.
PICKING FOR DRYING Summer.
DRYING METHODS Flowers: press or air dry by hanging or standing in container without water. Seed-heads: air dry by hanging or standing.

Chamaerops **Dwarf fan palm**
Trunkless palm trees. Leaves are fan-like with between 12 and 15 blades. The leaf stalks are spiny. Last very well when cut.
AVAILABILITY All year.
CONDITIONING (FRESH) Stand in deep water for several hours.
PICKING FOR DRYING All year.
DRYING METHODS Air dry by hanging.

Cheiranthus **Wallflower**
The well-known wallflowers come in a wide range of colours except blue. They are fragrant and last very well in water.
AVAILABILITY Spring.
CONDITIONING (FRESH) Slit and recut stems and then stand in deep water for several hours. Boiling-water treatment may be necessary.
PICKING FOR DRYING Spring.
DRYING METHODS Press individual flowers in flower press.

Chenopodium
Fig-leaved goose foot
The large flowering stems of this native plant dry very easily. Use the flowering side spikes as a filler, or use the whole stems to make a dramatic impact in large arrangements.
AVAILABILITY Summer.
CONDITIONING (FRESH) Boiling-water treatment and then stand in deep water for several hours.
PICKING FOR DRYING Autumn.
DRYING METHODS Air dry by standing in container without water.

Chionodoxa **Glory of the snow**
Short-stemmed bulbs with delightful starry flowers, blue or pink with a white throat.
AVAILABILITY Spring.
CONDITIONING (FRESH) Stand in deep water for several hours.
PICKING FOR DRYING Spring.
DRYING METHODS Press in flower press.

Choisya **Mexican orange**
Clusters of fragrant white flowers surrounded by glossy leaves forming a natural posy. The foliage is valuable in its own right. Leaves are ideal for preserving in glycerine; they turn a soft cream shade.
AVAILABILITY Flowers: summer. Foliage: all year.
CONDITIONING (FRESH) Scrape, slit and recut stems and then stand in deep water for several hours.
PICKING FOR DRYING Summer.
DRYING METHODS Preserve leaves by standing in glycerine.

Chrysanthemum
One of the most popular cut flowers with their large range of shapes and warm colours. They last a very long time in water. Some people do not like the smell of the bruised foliage. Also available as pot plants. Most chrysanthemums will not dry but *C. vulgare* air-dries well.
AVAILABILITY Autumn. All year from florists.
CONDITIONING (FRESH) Slit and recut stems and then stand in deep water for several hours.
PICKING FOR DRYING Summer.
DRYING METHODS Air dry by hanging. Press single flowers in flower press; dry double blooms in desiccant.

Cimifuga **Bugbane**
Long heads, almost like extended bottle brushes, with white or cream flowers. The long stems are a rich dark brown. Some have ferny leaves. Last reasonably well in water. Not suitable for drying.
AVAILABILITY Summer, autumn.
CONDITIONING (FRESH) Boiling-water treatment for stems and then stand in deep water for several hours.

Cladonia sp. **Silver lichen**
Lichen is extremely versatile and is used either dry or fresh. Can be used as a base for dried-flower arrangements or as exterior cladding for wreaths, trees or

any other shape. Alternatively, separate pieces can be wired and used like flowers. Conditioning not necessary for fresh arrangements.

PICKING FOR DRYING Any time.

DRYING METHODS Air dry in a box or basket.

Clarkia Godetia

Easy-to-grow annuals with brightly coloured flowers like funnels of crêpe paper in pink, red, purple, orange and white. Some of the flowers are semi-double or double. Leaves insignificant. Cut flowers last well in water.

AVAILABILITY Late spring, summer and autumn.

CONDITIONING (FRESH) Boiling-water treatment for stems and then stand in deep water for several hours.

PICKING FOR DRYING Summer.

DRYING METHODS Dry individual flowers in desiccant.

Clematis

Climbing and herbaceous plants. The smaller varieties make ideal trailing displays while the larger flowered varieties can be used singly. The herbaceous varieties last better in water. Seed-heads are also valuable for use in arrangements.

AVAILABILITY Spring, summer and autumn. Seed-heads: autumn.

CONDITIONING (FRESH) Slit and recut stems. Follow with boiling-water treatment and then stand in deep water for several hours.

PICKING FOR DRYING Late summer.

DRYING METHODS Air dry seed-heads by hanging. Press flowers in flower press.

Clivia Kaffir lily

Round heads of trumpet-shaped flowers in red and orange. Strap-shaped, glossy, dark green leaves. Last well in water.

AVAILABILITY Spring.

CONDITIONING (FRESH) Stand in deep water for several hours.

PICKING FOR DRYING Spring.

DRYING METHODS Dry individual flowers in desiccant.

Cobaea Cups and saucers

Annual or perennial climbing plants with large bell-shaped flowers of purple or pale green.

AVAILABILITY Summer, autumn.

CONDITIONING (FRESH) Stand in deep water for several hours.

PICKING FOR DRYING Summer and early autumn.

DRYING METHODS Dry individual flowers in desiccant.

Conifers

A wide range of evergreen trees and shrubs to give all-year foliage for decoration. The cones are also decorative in some species.

AVAILABILITY All year.

CONDITIONING (FRESH) Slit and recut stems then stand in deep water for several hours.

PICKING FOR DRYING All year.

DRYING METHODS As for fresh and then dry in arrangements, or preserve foliage by standing in glycerine.

Convallaria Lily-of-the-valley

Delicate little sprays of white bells of great charm. Excellent fragrance. A pink variety available. Good backing foliage. Last well in water.

AVAILABILITY Spring. Forced: all year.

CONDITIONING (FRESH) Stand in deep water for several hours.

PICKING FOR DRYING Spring.

DRYING METHODS Press flowers in flower press or dry in desiccant.

Coreopsis

Yellow daisy-like flowers with darker yellow eyes. They generally have long stems and deeply divided leaves. Several cultivars available with different shades of yellow and varying sizes of head and height.

AVAILABILITY Summer.

CONDITIONING (FRESH) Stand in

deep water for several hours.

PICKING FOR DRYING Summer.

DRYING METHODS Press flowers in flower press or dry in desiccant.

Cornus Dogwood

A large range of shrubs with good bark for winter arrangements. White or yellow flowers and bracts in spring. Good tints in autumn.

AVAILABILITY Bark: all year, particularly winter. Flowers: spring. Tints: autumn.

CONDITIONING (FRESH) Scrape, slit and recut stems. Follow with boiling-water treatment and then stand in deep water for several hours.

PICKING FOR DRYING Summer and autumn.

DRYING METHODS Press individual leaves in flower press.

Cortaderia selloana Pampas grass

Pick pink or cream pampas plumes the moment they are fully formed and spray them with hair lacquer to prevent the seeds from dropping. Arrange by themselves, or with other grasses, or separate the sections of each plume and use in smaller arrangements.

AVAILABILITY Autumn.

CONDITIONING (FRESH) Stand in deep water for several hours.

PICKING FOR DRYING Autumn.

DRYING METHODS Air dry by standing in container with a little water or preserve by standing in glycerine.

Corydalis

A genus of plants becoming very popular but difficult to obtain except for *C. lutea*. Small, delicate yellow flowers over filigree foliage.

AVAILABILITY Summer.

CONDITIONING (FRESH) Stand in deep water for several hours.

PICKING FOR DRYING Summer.

DRYING METHODS Press flowers and foliage in flower press.

Corylus **Hazel**

The familiar yellow catkins or lambs' tails of the hedgerow and coppice. The variety *C. avellana* 'Contorta' has delightful twisted stems. Also purple-leaved variety which is good for foliage. Dried branches can be coloured for use in festive decorations and arrangements.

AVAILABILITY Catkins: late winter, spring. Foliage: spring, summer.

CONDITIONING (FRESH) Slit and recut stems then stand in water for several hours.

PICKING FOR DRYING Winter.

DRYING METHODS Catkins: air dry by hanging or preserve by standing in glycerine. Stems: as for fresh and then air dry in position.

Cosmos

Tall fresh-looking plants with feathery foliage and flowers of white, pink, red and orange. *C. atrosanguineus* has unusually dark brown flowers and a smell reminiscent of hot chocolate. Last quite well in water.

AVAILABILITY Summer, autumn.

CONDITIONING (FRESH) Stand in deep water for several hours.

PICKING FOR DRYING Summer and autumn.

DRYING METHODS Press flowers and foliage in flower press.

Cotinus **Smoke tree**

Very valuable shrubs or trees with beautiful purple foliage. The leaves have a simple rounded shape which can be used to form a good background in arrange-ment. Also have good autumn tints. All varieties last reasonably well in water.

AVAILABILITY Summer, autumn.

CONDITIONING (FRESH) Scrape, slit and recut stems. Follow with boiling-water treatment and then stand in deep water for several hours.

PICKING FOR DRYING Autumn.

DRYING METHODS Air dry by hanging or press individual leaves in flower press.

Crocosmia **Montbretia**

Tall bulbous plants with sword-like leaves and arching sprays of bright orange flowers. Yellow varieties also available. Last quite well in water.

AVAILABILITY Late summer and autumn.

CONDITIONING (FRESH) Stand in deep water for several hours.

PICKING FOR DRYING Summer.

DRYING METHODS Seed pods: air dry by hanging. Flowers: dry in desiccants or press in flower press.

Crocus

Small bulbous plants bearing flowers shaped like chalices. Colours vary from cream and bright orange to blue and mauve. Also autumn forms. Before drying, wire each flower.

AVAILABILITY Late winter, spring and autumn.

CONDITIONING (FRESH) Stand in deep water for several hours.

PICKING FOR DRYING Early spring.

DRYING METHODS Dry with desiccant.

Cryptomeria **Japanese cedar**

Evergreen conifers with bronze, feathery foliage in winter and bright green foliage in spring. There are several varieties.

AVAILABILITY All year.

CONDITIONING (FRESH) Scrape, slit and recut stems and then stand in deep water for several hours.

PICKING FOR DRYING Summer.

DRYING METHODS As for fresh and then air dry in arrangement, or preserve by standing in glycerine. Air dry separate cones in basket.

Cuphea **Cigar flower**

Small, drooping tubular flowers in a variety of bright reds and yellow. Suitable for tiny arrange-ments. Not suitable for drying.

AVAILABILITY Summer. Green-house: all year.

CONDITIONING (FRESH) Stand in deep water for several hours.

Cyclamen **Sowbread**

A number of delicate species which will give almost all-year-round flowering in greenhouse and open garden. Also larger, more blowsy, florists' cyclamen as indoor pot plants. Colours available include white, mauve, pink and purple.

AVAILABILITY Species: autumn, winter and spring. Florists' plants: all year.

CONDITIONING (FRESH) Stand in deep water for several hours.

PICKING FOR DRYING All year.

DRYING METHODS Press smaller leaves in flower press.

Cymbidium

Aerial sprays of beautiful, exotic orchids in a large variety of colours with the exception of blue. They last extremely well in water.

AVAILABILITY All year from florists.

CONDITIONING (FRESH) Stand in deep water for several hours.

PICKING FOR DRYING All year.

DRYING METHODS Dry flowers in desiccant.

Cynara **Globe artichoke**

Versatile plants with good foliage and flower-heads. The latter are large and thistle-like and can be used in bud, in flower or in seed. The leaves are evergreen. The flower-heads can be dried.

AVAILABILITY Flowers: mid summer. Leaves: all year.

CONDITIONING (FRESH) Stand in deep water for several hours.

PICKING FOR DRYING Flowers: summer. Bracts: autumn.

DRYING METHODS Air dry by hanging or standing in container without water.

Cyperus **Papyrus, umbrella plant**

Plants with leaf-like bracts radiating from the top of the stem. Pot plants, but stems can be cut. Last well in water.

AVAILABILITY Summer.

CONDITIONING (FRESH) Stand in

deep water for several hours.
PICKING FOR DRYING Spring
DRYING METHODS Air dry by
hanging.

Cypripedium **Slipper orchid**
Curious orchids with slipper-like
pouches, surmounted by waxed
moustaches. Not so bright as
some of the other orchids.
AVAILABILITY Summer.
CONDITIONING (FRESH) Stand in
deep water for several hours.
PICKING FOR DRYING Summer.
DRYING METHODS Dry flowers in
desiccant.

Cytisus **Broom**
Shrubs covered with masses of
pea-like blooms. Available in
white, yellow, orange, pink and
red forms.
AVAILABILITY Spring.
CONDITIONING (FRESH) Slit and
recut stems. Follow with boiling-
water treatment and then stand
in deep water for several hours.
PICKING FOR DRYING Spring.
DRYING METHODS Stems (after
flowers dead): air dry by hanging or preserve by standing in
glycerine. Flowers: dry in
desiccant.

Dahlia
Half-hardy tuberous plants with a
great variety in flower shape and
colour. Colours include white,
red, mauve, yellow and orange.
Stems are long. They last well in
water, particularly pompons. For
drying, pick about four days
before flowers reach perfection.
AVAILABILITY Late summer and
autumn.
CONDITIONING (FRESH) Stand in
deep water for several hours.
PICKING FOR DRYING Autumn.
DRYING METHODS Air dry by
hanging, or dry with desiccant.

Daphne
Small slow-growing shrubs with
fragrant flowers mainly in red,
purple and white, also some in
yellow. *D. laureola* is evergreen.
Not suitable for drying.

AVAILABILITY Late winter, spring
and summer.
CONDITIONING (FRESH) Scrape,
slit and recut stems. Follow with
boiling-water treatment and then
stand in deep water for several
hours.

Delphinium
Tall spires of varying shades of
spurred, blue flowers with a dark
or white centre. Also white, pink
and purple varieties available.
Dwarf forms can now also be
found. They dry best in a cool,
dark, dry place. Pick when two-
thirds developed.
AVAILABILITY Summer, and
sometimes second flush in
autumn.
CONDITIONING (FRESH) Plug
hollow stems with cotton wool
and then stand in deep water for
several hours.
PICKING FOR DRYING Summer.
DRYING METHODS Air dry flowers
(remove leaves) by hanging or
standing in container in a little
water. Press individual flowers
and small sprays of foliage in
flower press.

Deutzia
Shrubs with clusters of small
single or double flowers in white
or pink. Some of the double
flowers are delightfully fringed.
Last quite well in water.
AVAILABILITY Late spring and
summer.
CONDITIONING (FRESH) Scrape,
slit and recut stems and then
stand in deep water for several
hours.
PICKING FOR DRYING Spring and
summer.
DRYING METHODS Dry small
sprays in desiccant.

Dianthus **Carnation, pink, sweet william**
One of the most popular of cut
flowers. White, pink and red
cultivars are available, some with
a contrasting eye. Usually
fragrant. All long lasting in water.
AVAILABILITY Summer and

autumn (old-fashioned pinks and
sweet williams early summer
only). All year from florists.
CONDITIONING (FRESH) Stand in
deep water for several hours.
PICKING FOR DRYING Summer.
DRYING METHODS Air dry small
double pinks by hanging. Dry
carnations in desiccant. Press
single pinks in flower press.

Dicentra **Bleeding heart**
Beautiful arching sprays of heart-
shaped flowers with ferny
foliage. Pink or white flowers.
Last well in water.
AVAILABILITY Spring, summer.
CONDITIONING (FRESH) Stand in
deep water for several hours.
PICKING FOR DRYING Spring and
summer.
DRYING METHODS Press individual
flowers in flower press or dry in
desiccant.

Digitalis **Foxglove**
These tall spires of purple bells
evoke high summer. There are
varieties with bells all round the
stems and other colours including
white and yellow.
AVAILABILITY Summer.
CONDITIONING (FRESH) Boiling-
water treatment after removing
longer leaves and then stand in
deep water for several hours.
PICKING FOR DRYING Summer.
DRYING METHODS Air dry seed-
heads by hanging. Dry individual
flowers in desiccant.

Doronicum **Leopard's bane**
Golden yellow daisies that
always seem to exude a fresh-
ness when they first appear in
spring. There are also double-
flowered varieties.
AVAILABILITY Spring.
CONDITIONING (FRESH) Stand in
deep water for several hours.
PICKING FOR DRYING Spring.
DRYING METHODS Press flowers
in flower press.

Dryandra
Australian evergreen shrubs
with orange and red flowers.

AVAILABILITY Spring.
CONDITIONING (FRESH) Scrape, slit and recut stems and then stand in deep water for several hours.
PICKING FOR DRYING Summer.
DRYING METHODS Air dry by hanging.

Dryopteris Male fern
Fern fronds press very easily and, because they grow in a two-dimensional way, they look perfectly natural when used pressed in arrangements.
AVAILABILITY Summer.
CONDITIONING (FRESH) Boiling-water treatment and then stand in deep water for several hours.
PICKING FOR DRYING Summer.
DRYING METHODS Air dry flat or press between newspaper under carpet where there is no traffic.

Echinops Globe thistle
Popular border plants with spiny spherical flowers much loved by bees. The commonest globe thistle has blue flowers but there are light green and white varieties. Tall and last very well in water. For drying, pick before the flower develops fully.
AVAILABILITY Summer.
CONDITIONING (FRESH) Stand in deep water for several hours. Boiling-water treatment when young.
PICKING FOR DRYING Summer.
DRYING METHODS Air dry by hanging or preserve mature flowers in glycerine.

Echium Viper's bugloss
Wild plants sometimes grown in gardens. Coils of blue flowers with red stamens. The leaves and stems are covered with small spines that get into the hands. Cultivated garden hybrids give a greater range of colours. Not suitable for drying.
AVAILABILITY Summer.
CONDITIONING (FRESH) Boiling-water treatment for stems and then stand in deep water for several hours.

Elaeagnus
Evergreen shrubs valuable for their foliage. *E. pungens* 'Maculata' and *E.* × *ebbingei* 'Gilt Edge' have excellent gold and green foliage and *E. angustifolia* and *E. commutata* have good silver foliage. To preserve, add green dye to the glycerine to "help" the colour.
AVAILABILITY All year.
CONDITIONING (FRESH) Hammer woody stems then stand in deep water for several hours.
PICKING FOR DRYING Summer.
DRYING METHODS Preserve by standing in glycerine.

Epilobium Willow herb
Wild or garden plants with spires of dark rosy-red flowers. Some species have very tall stems. Wild forms can be a menace if grown in the garden.
AVAILABILITY Summer.
CONDITIONING (FRESH) Boiling-water treatment and then stand in deep water for several hours. Wilt unless dealt with straight after picking.
PICKING FOR DRYING Summer.
DRYING METHODS Press individual flowers in flower press.

Eremurus Foxtail lily
Very tall, airy spikes of star-like flowers. Colours are white, pink or yellow. Some species are fragrant. Last well in water.
AVAILABILITY Summer.
CONDITIONING (FRESH) Stand in deep water for several hours.
PICKING FOR DRYING Summer.
DRYING METHODS Press individual flowers in flower press or dry in desiccant.

Erica Heath
Small shrubby plants useful both for the colour of their flowers and their foliage. There are always some varieties in flower all year. Flower colour varies from white to pink, mauve and purple. The leaves are of varying shades of green and gold. Even the rust brown seed-heads are attractive.

AVAILABILITY All year.
CONDITIONING (FRESH) Slit and recut stems and then stand in deep water for several hours.
PICKING FOR DRYING Summer.
DRYING METHODS Air dry by standing in container in a little water.

Erodium Stork's bill, heron's bill
Small, geranium-like flowers in pink and white varieties. The leaves and flowers press well.
AVAILABILITY Summer.
CONDITIONING (FRESH) Stand in deep water for several hours.
PICKING FOR DRYING Summer.
DRYING METHODS Press in flower press.

Eryngium Sea holly
Very spiky but very decorative plants in which even the flowers have spines. Colours are mainly blue but there are also green and white varieties. Some are a very airy maze of branches, others are more compact.
AVAILABILITY Summer, autumn.
CONDITIONING (FRESH) Stand in deep water for several hours.
PICKING FOR DRYING Late summer.
DRYING METHODS Air dry by hanging or preserve by standing in glycerine.

Escallonia
Late-flowering shrubs with arching stems covered with clusters of starry flowers in shades of pink, red and white. Glossy evergreen foliage. Last quite well in water.
AVAILABILITY Late summer and autumn.
CONDITIONING (FRESH) Scrape, slit and recut stems and then stand in deep water for several hours.
PICKING FOR DRYING Summer and autumn.
DRYING METHODS Flowers: dry in desiccant or press in flower press. Leaves: preserve by standing in glycerine.

Eucalyptus **Gum tree**
Very valuable for their ever-green greyish-silver foliage. Their very airy white flowers can also be attractive in arrangements. Long lasting in water.
AVAILABILITY Foliage: all year. Flowers: late autumn, early winter.
CONDITIONING (FRESH) Scrape, slit and recut stems and then stand in deep water for several hours.
PICKING FOR DRYING Summer.
DRYING METHODS Air dry by hanging, or preserve by standing in glycerine.

Euonymus **Spindle**
The deciduous spindles are valuable for their autumn colour and their red berries which open like a cardinal's hat. The ever-greens are valuable for their glossy foliage of which there are good variegated forms. Not suitable for drying.
AVAILABILITY Autumn for tints and berries. All year for ever-green foliage.
CONDITIONING (FRESH) Scrape, slit and recut stems and then stand in deep water for several hours.

Euphorbia **Spurge**
Valuable yellow- and green-leaved plants varying in height from short to tall. Long lasting in water. They also include the red-bracted pot plant poinsettia. Exude a caustic white sap. Not suitable for drying.
AVAILABILITY Spring and summer. Winter for poinsettia.
CONDITIONING (FRESH) Staunch the sap with a naked flame or fine sand. Stand in deep water for several hours.

Eustoma **Prairie gentian**
Beautiful trumpets of delicately arching purple flowers.
AVAILABILITY Summer only, from florists.
CONDITIONING (FRESH) Boiling-water treatment for stems and then stand in deep water for several hours.
DRYING METHODS Dry flowers in desiccant.

Fagus **Beech**
Valuable shiny foliage in either green or copper. The nut capsules are an interesting shape and can also be useful.
AVAILABILITY Foliage: spring and summer. Fruit: autumn.
CONDITIONING (FRESH) Scrape, slit and recut stems and then stand in deep water for several hours. Boiling-water treatment when young.
PICKING FOR DRYING Summer.
DRYING METHODS Air dry flat or press between newspaper under carpet where there is no traffic or preserve by standing in glycerine. Air dry nuts in basket.

Fatsia
Large, glossy, dark green leaves, deeply lobed like the fingers on a hand. Valuable for foliage decorations. Long lasting in water. Leaves preserved in glycerine become dark brown.
AVAILABILITY Summer.
CONDITIONING (FRESH) Slit and recut stems and then stand in deep water for several hours.
PICKING FOR DRYING Summer.
DRYING METHODS Air dry flat or press between newspaper under carpet where there is no traffic or preserve by standing in glycerine.

Ferns
A wide range of shapes and textures; some filigree, others strap-like. The fronds also have quite a range of different greens. They last well in water once they are cut.
AVAILABILITY Spring to autumn.
CONDITIONING (FRESH) Char stem ends with naked flame and stand in deep water for several hours. Boiling-water treatment when young.
PICKING FOR DRYING Spring and summer.

Ficus **Rubber plant, weeping fig**
Foliage plants with glossy, leathery leaves of different sizes. Some useful for cutting. Not suitable for drying.
AVAILABILITY All year.
CONDITIONING (FRESH) Boiling-water treatment and then stand in deep water for several hours.

Foeniculum **Common fennel**
The delicate seed formation of fennel looks rather like dill when dry and can be used for its feathery texture.
AVAILABILITY Summer.
CONDITIONING (FRESH) Boiling-water treatment and then stand in deep water for several hours.
PICKING FOR DRYING Summer.
DRYING METHODS Air dry by hanging or preserve seed-heads by standing in glycerine.

Forsythia **Golden-bell**
Shrubs with starry yellow flowers which are out just before the leaves appear. Can be cut in winter for forcing long before the flowers normally appear. Last quite well in water.
AVAILABILITY Spring. Winter if forced.
CONDITIONING (FRESH) Scrape, slit and recut stems and then stand in deep water for several hours. Boiling-water treatment for forcing flowers.
PICKING FOR DRYING Spring.
DRYING METHODS Press individual flowers in flower press or dry in desiccant.

Freesia
One of the most scented of cut flowers. The stems of waxy flowers open one or two at a time and are available in a wide variety of colours. They last well in water.
AVAILABILITY Summer. All year from florists.

CONDITIONING (FRESH) Stand in deep water for several hours.
PICKING FOR DRYING Summer.
DRYING METHODS Dry with desiccant or press in flower press.

Fritillaria **Fritillary, crown imperial**
A large genus of bulbous plants, the most common of which is the snake's-head fritillary with its solitary, nodding purple or white chequered bells. Crown imperials are much larger with a cluster of yellow or orange-red bells on the top of the stem, and leaves that look like a pineapple. Not suitable for drying.
AVAILABILITY Spring.
CONDITIONING (FRESH) Stand in deep water for several hours.

Fuchsia
Small shrubs with pendulous flowers, usually bell-shaped, in a range of pinks, purples and reds. Some forms have variegated foliage. Only a few are hardy.
AVAILABILITY Summer, autumn.
CONDITIONING (FRESH) Scrape, slit and recut stems and then stand in deep water for several hours.
PICKING FOR DRYING Summer and autumn.
DRYING METHODS Press flowers in flower press or dry in desiccant.

Gaillardia **Blanket flower**
Bright daisy-like flowers in glowing shades of red, yellow and orange. Double and single forms. Last well in water.
AVAILABILITY Summer, autumn.
CONDITIONING (FRESH) Stand in deep water for several hours.
PICKING FOR DRYING Summer and autumn.
DRYING METHODS Press flowers in flower press.

Garrya **Silk tassel bush**
Valuable evergreen shrubs that have flowers in the form of long, silky, green tassels throughout

the winter at a time when there is not much else around. Last well in water.
AVAILABILITY Winter.
CONDITIONING (FRESH) Scrape, slit and recut stems and then stand in deep water for several hours.
PICKING FOR DRYING Winter.
DRYING METHODS Preserve by standing in glycerine when tassels mature.

Genista **Broom**
Arching branches of yellow pea-shaped flowers. Some fragrant species. Last quite well in water.
AVAILABILITY Early summer.
CONDITIONING (FRESH) Slit and recut stems and then stand in deep water for several hours.
PICKING FOR DRYING Summer.
DRYING METHODS Stems (after flowers dead): air dry by hanging or preserve by standing in glycerine. Flowers: dry in desiccant.

Gentiana **Gentian**
Upright trumpets of bright blue. The majority are short-stemmed but there are some bigger subjects, such as *G. asclepiadea*, which is up to 60cm (2ft). Some species have white varieties.
AVAILABILITY Spring to late autumn.
CONDITIONING (FRESH) Stand in water in a warm, light place to open fully.
PICKING FOR DRYING Autumn.
DRYING METHODS Dry with desiccant.

Geranium **Cranesbill**
Popular herbaceous perennials with saucer-shaped flowers. There is a vast number of species available in colours ranging from the basic blue, mauve and purple, to red, pink and white, many having contrasting veining. Vary in height from small to tall. Not long lasting. The seed-heads are attractive.
AVAILABILITY Late spring to autumn.

CONDITIONING (FRESH) Stand in deep water for several hours.
PICKING FOR DRYING Late summer to autumn.
DRYING METHODS Press individual flowers and leaves in flower press.

Gerbera **Transvaal daisy**
Brightly coloured, daisy-like flowers in cream, yellow, orange, red, pink or purple. Tender and eye-catching. Last well in water. Not suitable for drying.
AVAILABILITY All year from florist.
CONDITIONING (FRESH) Boiling-water treatment for stems and then stand in deep water for several hours.

Geum **Avens**
Herbaceous perennials with brilliant red, yellow or orange flowers. There are single, semi-double or double flowers, the general shape being circular. Tend to hang their heads.
AVAILABILITY Late spring and summer.
CONDITIONING (FRESH) Boiling-water treatment for stems and then stand in deep water for several hours.
PICKING FOR DRYING Late spring and summer.
DRYING METHODS Press single forms in flower press and dry semi-double and double forms in desiccant.

Gladiolus **Sword lily**
These are well-known bulbous plants with tall, slightly arching stems of brightly coloured flowers. The leaves are long and sword-like. Most colours are available except true blue. Last well in water.
AVAILABILITY Summer, autumn.
CONDITIONING (FRESH) Remove top buds, slit and recut stems and then stand in deep water for several hours.
PICKING FOR DRYING Summer and autumn.
DRYING METHODS Dry smaller flowers in desiccant.

Glaucium **Horned-poppy**

Bright yellow or orange-red, papery flowers set off against a greyish stem and foliage. Long curved seed pods from whence comes its English name. Not suitable for drying.

AVAILABILITY Summer, autumn.
CONDITIONING (FRESH) Stand in deep water for several hours.

Gomphrena

Of the many species *G. globosa* is the main one in cultivation. Annuals with globular flowers of white, yellow, orange, red, pink and purple. Flowers are "everlasting" and can be easily dried.

AVAILABILITY Summer.
CONDITIONING (FRESH) Stand in deep water for several hours.
PICKING FOR DRYING Summer.
DRYING METHODS Air dry by hanging.

Grevillea

Tender shrubs useful for their evergreen, fern-like foliage and petal-less flowers in yellow and red. Last well when cut.

AVAILABILITY Summer.
CONDITIONING (FRESH) Scrape, slit and recut stems and then stand in deep water for several hours.
PICKING FOR DRYING Summer.
DRYING METHODS Air dry leaves by hanging or preserve by standing in glycerine.

Grimmia **Bun moss**

Brilliant green mounds of moss make an ideal base for dried-flower trees or for "landscape" arrangements or basket displays of bright spring flowers. Conditioning not necessary for fresh arrangements.

PICKING FOR DRYING Summer.
DRYING METHODS Air dry in basket or box.

Griselinia

Evergreen shrubs which are valuable for their foliage, particularly in the variegated forms. All are long lasting.

AVAILABILITY All year.
CONDITIONING (FRESH) Scrape, slit and recut stems and then stand in deep water for several hours.
PICKING FOR DRYING All year.
DRYING METHODS Preserve by standing in glycerine.

Gypsophila **Baby's breath**

Marvellous airy plants with fine wiry stems and little puffs of dainty white flowers. Pink varieties also available. Long lasting in water.

AVAILABILITY Summer.
CONDITIONING (FRESH) Stand in deep water for several hours.
PICKING FOR DRYING Summer.
DRYING METHODS Air dry by standing in container with a little water or hanging. Press flowers in flower press or dry in desiccant.

Hamamelis **Witch hazel**

Deciduous shrubs with flowers made up of clusters of spidery, strap-like yellow petals on the naked branches. The flowers are fragrant. Autumn foliage is useful for pressed-flower pictures.

AVAILABILITY Late winter.
CONDITIONING (FRESH) Scrape, slit and recut stems then stand in deep water for several hours.
PICKING FOR DRYING Autumn.
DRYING METHODS Press individual leaves in flower press.

Hebe **Shrubby veronica**

A group of mainly New Zealand evergreen shrubs with dense spikes of blue, white or pink flowers. Some are scented. A few species are hardy; the rest need winter protection.

AVAILABILITY Summer, autumn.
CONDITIONING (FRESH) Scrape, slit and recut stems. Follow with boiling-water treatment and then stand in deep water for several hours.
PICKING FOR DRYING Summer and autumn.
DRYING METHODS Preserve leaves by standing in glycerine.

Hedera **Ivy**

Creeping foliage plants with distinctive leaves. There is considerable variation in size of leaf and the markings found on them. There are many variegated forms. Long lasting. Also available as pot plants. Add a little green dye to glycerine when preserving to maintain colour.

AVAILABILITY All year.
CONDITIONING Slit and recut stems and then stand in deep water for several hours. Boiling-water treatment when young.
PICKING FOR DRYING All year.
DRYING METHODS Press in flower press or preserve by standing in glycerine.

Helenium **Sneezeweed**

Clusters of yellow, daisy-like flowers on top of medium-length stems. Orange and brown varieties also available. Last quite well in water.

AVAILABILITY Summer, autumn.
CONDITIONING (FRESH) Slit and recut stems and then stand in deep water for several hours.
PICKING FOR DRYING Summer and autumn.
DRYING METHODS Dry flowers in desiccant.

Helianthus **Sunflower**

Very tall, yellow daisy-like flowers. The well-known annual sunflower has a large, dark central disc. The perennial flowers are all much smaller.

AVAILABILITY Autumn.
CONDITIONING (FRESH) Boiling-water treatment and then stand in deep water for several hours.
PICKING FOR DRYING Autumn.
DRYING METHODS Dry smaller flowers in desiccant.

Helichrysum
Everlasting flower

Very colourful daisy-like flowers with papery bracts instead of petals. They can be yellow, brown, orange, red or pink in colour. Fresh flowers last very well and are good dried.

AVAILABILITY Summer.
CONDITIONING (FRESH) Stand in deep water for several hours.
PICKING FOR DRYING Summer before fully open.
DRYING METHODS Air dry by hanging.

Helipterum Sunray, everlasting daisy

These delicate daisies are really fresh-looking when dried, especially when grouped in bunches in an arrangement. Extremely versatile flowers, they look good in large and small arrangements, by themselves or mixed with other dried flowers.
AVAILABILITY Summer.
CONDITIONING (FRESH) Stand in deep water for several hours.
PICKING FOR DRYING Summer before fully open.
DRYING METHODS Air dry by hanging.

Helleborus Christmas rose, Lenten rose, hellebore

An interesting range of saucer-shaped, winter flowers varying in colour from the white Christmas rose through to the plum-coloured and spotted Lenten roses. The green and stinking hellebores tend to have smaller, more cup-shaped flowers.
AVAILABILITY Winter, spring.
CONDITIONING (FRESH) Prick the stems with a pin. Follow with boiling-water treatment and then stand in deep water for several hours.
PICKING FOR DRYING Winter and spring.
DRYING METHODS Dry flowers in desiccant, preserve leaves by standing in glycerine. Press leaves and flowers in flower press.

Heracleum Giant hogweed

Very tall plants with cartwheels of white flowers, like giant cow parsley. Sap can cause skin irritation. Seed-heads can be used dried.
AVAILABILITY Late summer.

CONDITIONING (FRESH) Boiling-water treatment and then stand in deep water for several hours.
PICKING FOR DRYING Autumn.
DRYING METHODS Air dry by standing in container with a little water or preserve by standing in glycerine.

Heuchera Coral flower

Sprays of airy flowers on thin stems. Colours include white, cream, pink and red. Last quite well in water.
AVAILABILITY Summer.
CONDITIONING (FRESH) Stand in deep water for several hours.
PICKING FOR DRYING Summer.
DRYING METHODS Press individual leaves and sprays in flower press or dry sprays in desiccant.

Hibiscus

Exotic trumpet-shaped flowers borne on tender shrubs and perennials. Each flower lasts only a day, and is then replaced by more. They are available in the full range of tropical colours. Not suitable for drying.
AVAILABILITY Late summer and autumn.
CONDITIONING (FRESH) Slit and recut stems, follow with boiling-water treatment and then stand in deep water for several hours.

Hippeastrum Amaryllis

Large lily-type flowers radiating from a tall stem. White, pink or red. Strap-like leaves. Bulbous. Not suitable for drying.
AVAILABILITY Winter, spring.
CONDITIONING (FRESH) Fill hollow stem with water, plug end with cotton wool and stand in deep water for several hours. If head is heavy, support with cane pushed up hollow stem.

Hosta Plantain lily

Marvellous for both their foliage and spikes of flowers. The leaves are large and heart-shaped in varying shades of green and steely blue. There are also many variegated forms. The flowers

are either white, lilac-blue or purple. Long lasting in water.
AVAILABILITY Summer, autumn.
CONDITIONING (FRESH) Submerge leaves for a few minutes and then stand in deep water for several hours.
PICKING FOR DRYING Summer.
DRYING METHODS Dry flat or press between newspaper under carpet where there is no traffic or in flower press. Preserve foliage by immersing in glycerine.

Humulus Hops

Flowers have greenish bracts. Pick well before the heads ripen. Otherwise, they will fall to pieces as they dry. Hops tend to lose their colour quickly once dry.
AVAILABILITY Flowers: summer.
CONDITIONING (FRESH) Slit and recut stems and then stand in deep water for several hours.
PICKING FOR DRYING Early autumn.
DRYING METHODS Air dry by hanging or preserve by standing in glycerine.

Hyacinthoides Bluebell

Arching stems of blue bells and strap-like leaves. Pink and white varieties also available. Fragrant.
AVAILABILITY Spring.
CONDITIONING (FRESH) Stand in deep water for several hours.
PICKING FOR DRYING Spring.
DRYING METHODS Dry individual flowers in desiccant.

Hyacinthus Hyacinth

Bulbous plants with spikes of very fragrant flowers in blue, white and pink.
AVAILABILITY Spring. Winter if forced.
CONDITIONING (FRESH) Stand in deep water for several hours. Support stems with wires.
PICKING FOR DRYING Spring.
DRYING METHODS Dry individual flowers in desiccant.

Hydrangea

Shrubs with large mops of flower-heads. White, blue,

mauve, pink and red. There are also varieties with pointed spikes of flowers and delicate lacecaps, with just a few large, sterile florets round the edge of tiny, fertile florets.

AVAILABILITY Summer, autumn.
CONDITIONING (FRESH) Slit and recut stems and then stand in deep water for several hours.
PICKING FOR DRYING Autumn.
DRYING METHODS Air dry by hanging or by standing in container with a little water when bracts feel papery. Preserve leaves by standing in glycerine. Press individual bracts in flower press.

Hypericum St John's wort

Shrubs and sub-shrubs with saucer-shaped, golden-yellow flowers. Several good fruiting forms including *H. calycinum* (rose of sharon).

AVAILABILITY Summer, autumn.
CONDITIONING (FRESH) Slit and recut stems and stand in deep water for several hours. Boiling-water treatment when young.
PICKING FOR DRYING Summer and autumn.
DRYING METHODS Press individual flowers in flower press.

Iberis Candytuft

Flat or domed heads of white flowers. Also pink and mauve varieties. Short-stemmed. Last very well in water. Seed-heads can be dried on plant.

AVAILABILITY Spring.
CONDITIONING (FRESH) Stand in deep water for several hours.
PICKING FOR DRYING Summer
DRYING METHODS Preserve seed-heads by standing in glycerine.

Ilex Holly

Glossy prickly-leaved shrubs or trees useful for their foliage and bright red berries borne in mid-winter. There are variegated and yellow-berried forms. Flowers are insignificant, but leaves last well in water.

AVAILABILITY Winter.

CONDITIONING (FRESH) Scrape, slit and recut stems and then stand in deep water for several hours.
PICKING FOR DRYING Summer.
DRYING METHODS Preserve by standing in glycerine.

Iris Flag

Flowers that cover a long season starting with *I. unguicularis* in early winter, followed by the tiny reticulatas in winter and spring, and finally the taller species in summer. Some are scented. Not suitable for drying.

AVAILABILITY Winter, spring and summer. All year from florists.
CONDITIONING (FRESH) Stand in deep water for several hours.

Ixia

Slender-stemmed bulbous plants with several star-like flowers per stem. A large range of colours including bluish-green. Last well in water. Tender.

AVAILABILITY Spring.
CONDITIONING (FRESH) Stand in deep water for several hours.
PICKING FOR DRYING Spring.
DRYING METHODS Press flowers in flower press.

Ixodia

The creamy white heads of the little, waxy daisy flowers are extremely pretty and have a very fresh look when dried. They mix well in arrangements with all sorts of old-fashioned "country" or woodland flowers.

AVAILABILITY Summer.
CONDITIONING (FRESH) Stand in deep water for several hours.
PICKING FOR DRYING Summer.
DRYING METHODS Air dry by hanging.

Jasminum Jasmine

Both winter and summer forms. The former has starry yellow flowers on arching stems. In the summer there are white forms which are extremely fragrant. There are also yellow and pink forms available in summer.

AVAILABILITY Winter, summer.
CONDITIONING (FRESH) Stand in deep water for several hours immediately after cutting stems.
PICKING FOR DRYING Winter and summer.
DRYING METHODS Press individual flowers in flower press.

Juniperus Juniper

Columnar or spreading ever-green conifers giving all-year-round foliage. Colour varies from green and blue to gold. The dwarf *J. communis* 'Compressa' is small enough for the whole tree to be used if potted.

AVAILABILITY All year.
CONDITIONING (FRESH) Scrape, slit and recut stems and then stand in deep water for several hours.
PICKING FOR DRYING Summer.
DRYING METHODS Dry separate cones in box.

Kalanchoe

Tender succulents usually grown as pot plants that flower through-out the year. Flowers can be white, pink, red or yellow. Not suitable for drying.

AVAILABILITY All year.
CONDITIONING Stand flowers in deep water for several hours.

Kniphofia Red-hot poker, torch lily

Tall upright stems with a colour-ful spike of red, orange or yellow flowers. They are not long lasting in water.

AVAILABILITY Summer, autumn.
CONDITIONING (FRESH) Stand in deep water for several hours.
PICKING FOR DRYING Summer and autumn.
DRYING METHODS Dry individual flowers in desiccant.

Kochia Burning bush

Fine-leaved plants that are said to resemble guards' "busbies". They are bright green turning dark red in autumn.

AVAILABILITY Summer, autumn.
CONDITIONING (FRESH) Stand in

deep water for several hours.
PICKING FOR DRYING Summer and autumn.
DRYING METHODS Air dry by hanging.

Laburnum Golden chain, golden rain

Trees with pendulous tassels of yellow pea-like flowers. Seeds are very poisonous.
AVAILABILITY Early summer.
CONDITIONING (FRESH) Boiling-water treatment for stems and then stand in deep water for several hours.
PICKING FOR DRYING Summer.
DRYING METHODS Press individual flowers in flower press.

Lachenalia Cape cowslip

Tender bulbous plants with a spike of numerous bell-shaped flowers in yellow, orange and red. Normally grown in greenhouse. Last well in water.
AVAILABILITY Winter and spring.
CONDITIONING (FRESH) Stand in deep water for several hours.
PICKING FOR DRYING Winter.
DRYING METHODS Press individual flowers in flower press or dry in desiccant.

Larix Larch

Deciduous conifers best in spring when the light green, new growth is supplemented by the newly forming cones which are pink or red. Branches with sprays of small cones can be used in winter.
AVAILABILITY Foliage: spring. Cones: winter.
CONDITIONING (FRESH) Scrape, slit and recut stems and then stand in deep water for several hours. Boiling-water treatment when young.
PICKING FOR DRYING Autumn.
DRYING METHODS Air dry branches by hanging and separate cones in basket.

Lathyrus Everlasting pea, sweet pea

Sweet peas are justly well loved for their grace and fresh smell. There is now a vast range of cultivars from which to choose. Not all are fragrant. The long-stemmed flowers last quite well in water. There are also many other species which are perennial but these lack scent and have restricted colour range. Not suitable for drying.
AVAILABILITY Summer.
CONDITIONING (FRESH) Stand in deep water for several hours.

Lavandula Lavender

Grey-leaved shrubs with spikes of pale purple flowers on long stems. The plants are very strongly scented. There are darker purple and white forms. Pick flowers just as buds begin to open; any later and flowers will drop off. Drying them fast in a warm airing cupboard helps to fix the flowers.
AVAILABILITY Summer, autumn.
CONDITIONING (FRESH) Stand in deep water for several hours.
PICKING FOR DRYING Summer.
DRYING METHODS Air dry by hanging.

Lavatera Mallow

Annuals with bright pink or white trumpets. Also perennial species but these are duller and not so interesting. Last reasonably well in water after cutting.
AVAILABILITY Summer, autumn.
CONDITIONING (FRESH) Boiling-water treatment for stems and then stand in deep water for several hours.
PICKING FOR DRYING Summer and autumn.
DRYING METHODS Press flowers in flower press or dry in desiccant.

Leptospermum Manuka, tea tree

Popular New Zealand shrub in mild conditions. Branches are covered with masses of small white, pink or red flowers.
AVAILABILITY Summer.
CONDITIONING (FRESH) Scrape, slit and recut stems and then stand in deep water for several hours.
PICKING FOR DRYING Summer.
DRYING METHODS Air dry flower stems by standing in container in a little water.

Leucodendron Leucodendron, tolbos, topbrush, silver bush

These woody seeding cones, often growing on stems with pale greeny-silver leaves, are like flowers and have a strong form that looks very well in autumnal-coloured arrangements.
AVAILABILITY Summer.
CONDITIONING (FRESH) Slit and recut stems and then stand in deep water for several hours.
PICKING FOR DRYING Summer.
DRYING METHODS Air dry hanging or standing in container without water.

Liatris Gayfeather

Several species of long, purple spikes of feathery flowers. Unusual in that they flower from tip of spike downwards. For drying, pick when most flowers open. Last well in water.
AVAILABILITY Summer, autumn.
CONDITIONING (FRESH) Stand in deep water for several hours.
PICKING FOR DRYING Summer.
DRYING METHODS Air dry by hanging.

Ligustrum Privet

Evergreen shrubs useful for their foliage. Available in golden colours as well as green. White flowers with a scent that some find nasty, others attractive. Black berries in autumn.
AVAILABILITY All year.
CONDITIONING (FRESH) Slit and recut stems and then stand in deep water for several hours.
PICKING FOR DRYING Summer.
DRYING METHODS Preserve green form by standing in glycerine.

Lilium Lily

Beautiful, well-loved flowers shaped either like large trumpets

or turks' caps with curled back petals. Large range of colours (except blue), either plain or spotted. Many are fragrant. Last very well in water.
AVAILABILITY Summer and autumn. All year from florists.
CONDITIONING (FRESH) Stand in deep water for several hours.
PICKING FOR DRYING Summer and autumn.
DRYING METHODS Flowers: dry with desiccant or press in flower press. Seed-heads: air dry by hanging.

Limonium Sea lavender, statice, lamb's tail
Brightly coloured flowers that last very well in water. A large range of colours is available, with blue, yellow and pink predominating.
AVAILABILITY Summer and autumn. All year from florists.
CONDITIONING (FRESH) Stand in deep water for several hours.
PICKING FOR DRYING Summer.
DRYING METHODS Air dry hanging or standing in container without water.

Lonicera Honeysuckle
Well-known and well-loved climbing plants which produce very heavily scented flowers, particularly strong in the evening. Various colours are available, including yellow, orange and red. There are also variegated-leaved forms. Do not last very long in water after cutting.
AVAILABILITY Summer, autumn.
CONDITIONING (FRESH) Stand in deep water for several hours.
PICKING FOR DRYING Summer and autumn.
DRYING METHODS Press flowers in flower press.

Lunaria Honesty
Biennial and perennial plants that do double service. In spring they have purple or white flowers. There are varieties with good variegated foliage. Later they have almost transparent, silky seed-cases that are extremely useful in dried arrangements.
AVAILABILITY Flowers: spring. Seed-cases: autumn.
CONDITIONING (FRESH) Stand in deep water for several hours.
PICKING FOR DRYING Autumn.
DRYING METHODS Dry on the plant and remove outer scales or air dry by hanging or standing in container with no water. Preserve green seed-cases by standing in glycerine.

Lupinus Lupin
Old-fashioned, cottage garden plants with spires of pea-like flowers. Large number of cultivars available in a good range of colours including yellow, blue, white, pink and orange. Peppery scent. Last very well in water.
AVAILABILITY Summer.
CONDITIONING (FRESH) Fill hollow stems with water and plug with cotton wool, or boiling-water treatment. Stand in deep water for several hours.
PICKING FOR DRYING Summer.
DRYING METHODS Dry individual flowers in desiccant or press in flower press.

Lysimachia Yellow loosestrife
Spikes of bright yellow, cup-shaped flowers. The spikes are clothed with whorls of flowers backed by leaves. Last quite well in water.
AVAILABILITY Summer.
CONDITIONING (FRESH) Stand in deep water for several hours.
PICKING FOR DRYING Summer.
DRYING METHODS Press individual flowers in flower press.

Lythrum Purple loosestrife
Tall herbaceous plants that have spires of brilliant purple flowers. They do not last very long in water but add a good vertical emphasis, with a splash of strong colour, to arrangements. Not suitable for drying.
AVAILABILITY Late summer and autumn.
CONDITIONING (FRESH) Boiling-water treatment for stems and then stand in deep water for several hours.

Magnolia
Deciduous and evergreen shrubs and trees with predominantly white flowers, flushed sometimes with pink. Some varieties are scented.
AVAILABILITY Spring and summer.
CONDITIONING (FRESH) Scrape, slit and recut stems. Follow with boiling-water treatment and then stand in deep water for several hours.
PICKING FOR DRYING Spring and summer.
DRYING METHODS Leaves: preserve by standing in glycerine. Flowers: dry with desiccant.

Mahonia Oregon grape
Evergreen shrubs with glossy, spiny leaves and spikes of fragrant yellow flowers. Blue-black fruit in autumn.
AVAILABILITY Foliage: all year. Flowers: winter, spring. Fruit: autumn.
CONDITIONING (FRESH) Scrape, slit and recut stems and then stand in deep water for several hours.
PICKING FOR DRYING Summer.
DRYING METHODS Preserve by standing in glycerine.

Malus Apple, crab apple
Deciduous trees with pink-tinged blossom in spring, and shiny green, yellow or red apples of various sizes in the autumn. Some have decorative foliage.
AVAILABILITY Blossom: spring. Foliage: summer, autumn. Fruit: autumn.
CONDITIONING (FRESH) Scrape, slit and recut stems and then stand in deep water for several hours.
PICKING FOR DRYING Spring and autumn.
DRYING METHODS Air dry fruits by standing branches in container in a little water. Press flowers in flower press.

Matteucia
Ostrich feather fern
The dried fronds of this beautiful fern, which grows like a shuttlecock, can be used like fresh fern.
AVAILABILITY Summer.
CONDITIONING (FRESH) Boiling-water treatment, when young, and stand in deep water for several hours.
PICKING FOR DRYING Summer.
DRYING METHODS Air dry flat or press between newspaper under carpet where there is no traffic.

Matthiola **Stock**
Annuals and biennials, which are among the most popular cut flowers, with small spired, soft-coloured, scented flowers. Good range of pink, purple, white, yellow and cream. Last quite well in water.
AVAILABILITY Summer. Florists: spring and summer.
CONDITIONING (FRESH) Stand in deep water for several hours.
PICKING FOR DRYING Summer.
DRYING METHODS Dry individual flowers in desiccant.

Miscanthus
Tall ornamental grasses valuable for their foliage and plumed seed-heads. Several variegated forms including one with horizontal yellow stripes on the leaves. The blue-green leaves and fronds dry to a beige colour.
AVAILABILITY Summer.
CONDITIONING (FRESH) Stand in deep water for several hours.
PICKING FOR DRYING Summer and autumn.
DRYING METHODS Air dry by hanging or by standing in container without water.

Moluccella **Bells of Ireland, shell flower**
Tall stems of green trumpets in which sit tiny white flowers. The green calyces continue long after the flower dies. Last very well in water. For drying, they should be picked just as the first flowers emerge.

AVAILABILITY Summer, autumn.
CONDITIONING (FRESH) Remove all leaves, follow with boiling-water treatment and then stand in deep water for several hours.
PICKING FOR DRYING Summer.
DRYING METHODS Remove all leaves and air dry by hanging or preserve by standing in glycerine.

Monarda **Bergamot**
Whorls of red, pink or white flowers that seem to spring from a pincushion at the top of the stem. Very aromatic foliage when crushed.
AVAILABILITY Summer, autumn.
CONDITIONING (FRESH) Stand in deep water for several hours.
PICKING FOR DRYING Summer and autumn.
DRYING METHODS Air dry flowers by hanging.

Muscari **Grape hyacinth**
Small-stemmed bulbs with spikes of varying shades of blue, scented flowers. White varieties also available.
AVAILABILITY Spring.
CONDITIONING (FRESH) Stand in deep water for several hours.
PICKING FOR DRYING Spring.
DRYING METHODS Dry flowers in desiccant.

Myosotis **Forget-me-not**
Short arching sprays of blue flowers. Last quite well in water.
AVAILABILITY Late spring and summer.
CONDITIONING (FRESH) Stand in deep water for several hours. Keep cool.
PICKING FOR DRYING Spring and summer.
DRYING METHODS Press in flower press.

Narcissus **Daffodil, jonquil**
Very popular spring bulbs with trumpets or cups coming from a disc of petals. Mainly yellow but white, orange and pink varieties are also available. In addition, there are many miniature forms

of daffodil including the jonquils. Many are fragrant.
AVAILABILITY Spring. Florists: winter and spring.
CONDITIONING (FRESH) Cut in bud. Stand in deep water for several hours.
PICKING FOR DRYING Spring.
DRYING METHODS Dry with desiccant, crystallize or press in flower press.

Nepeta **Catmint**
Airy stems of pale blue or mauve flowers set off against grey foliage. The foliage is fragrant, particularly when crushed. Last quite well in water.
AVAILABILITY Summer.
CONDITIONING (FRESH) Stand in deep water for several hours.
PICKING FOR DRYING Summer.
DRYING METHODS Air dry by hanging.

Nephrolepis **Ladder fern**
Evergreen ferns that are usually grown as pot plants. The cut fronds last well in water and can be pressed successfully.
AVAILABILITY All year.
CONDITIONING (FRESH) Stand in deep water for several hours.
PICKING FOR DRYING All year.
DRYING METHODS Press between newspaper under carpet where there is no traffic.

Nerine
Autumnal bulbous plants with clusters of pink trumpet-like flowers. Last very well in water.
AVAILABILITY Autumn.
CONDITIONING (FRESH) Stand in deep water for several hours.
PICKING FOR DRYING Autumn.
DRYING METHODS Dry individual flowers in desiccant.

Nicotiana **Tobacco plant**
Annual starry-flowered plants coming in a variety of colours, the greens being particularly important. Some varieties very fragrant, particularly after dark. Last well in water.
AVAILABILITY Summer, autumn.

CONDITIONING (FRESH) Stand in deep water for several hours.
PICKING FOR DRYING Summer and autumn.
DRYING METHODS Dry flowers in desiccant or press in flower press.

Nigella Love-in-a-mist
Hardy annuals with blue flowers and a collar of bright-green, feathery foliage. Last very well in water. The almost spherical seed-heads are very beautiful and dry easily. The flowers need to be placed in a warm airing cupboard or warming oven for best results.
AVAILABILITY Summer.
CONDITIONING (FRESH) Stand in deep water for several hours.
PICKING FOR DRYING Summer, early autumn.
DRYING METHODS Air dry seed-heads by hanging.

Ornithogalum Star of Bethlehem, Chincherinchee
Bulbs with either sprays or spikes of small white flowers. Last very well in water.
AVAILABILITY Spring. All year from florists.
CONDITIONING (FRESH) Stand in deep water for several hours.
PICKING FOR DRYING Spring.
DRYING METHODS Dry individual flowers in desiccant or press in flower press.

Osmunda Flowering fern, royal fern
Tall deciduous varieties of fern.
AVAILABILITY Summer.
CONDITIONING (FRESH) Stand in deep water for several hours. Boiling-water treatment, when young.
PICKING FOR DRYING Summer.
DRYING METHODS Air dry flat or press between newpaper under carpet where there is no traffiic.

Paeonia Paeony
Herbaceous or shrubby plants. Large bold flower-heads of red, white, yellow or pink. Can be single or double. Some varieties are also scented.
AVAILABILITY Summer.
CONDITIONING (FRESH) Boiling-water treatment and then stand in deep water for several hours.
PICKING FOR DRYING Summer.
DRYING METHODS Dry with desiccant, air dry by hanging or press petals in flower press.

Papaver Poppy
Brightly coloured flowers with tissue-like petals. Not long lasting in water: pick when bud showing colour.
AVAILABILITY Summer, autumn.
CONDITIONING (FRESH) Cut as buds open. Seal sappy stem over naked flame or boiling-water treatment and then stand in deep water for several hours.
PICKING FOR DRYING Summer.
DRYING METHODS Air dry seed-heads by hanging or preserve by standing in glycerine. Press flowers in flower press.

Pelargonium Geranium
Tender plants with very colourful heads of flowers in bright reds, pinks, purples and white. Some leaves are fragrant and others have good zonal markings.
AVAILABILITY Summer, autumn.
CONDITIONING (FRESH) Stand in deep water for several hours.
PICKING FOR DRYING Summer and autumn.
DRYING METHODS Press leaves and individual flowers in flower press.

Penstemon
Spikes of tubular flowers of bright or more subtle colours. Available in a range of red, pink, purple and blue. Do not last long in water.
AVAILABILITY Summer, autumn.
CONDITIONING (FRESH) Stand in deep water for several hours.
PICKING FOR DRYING Summer and autumn.
DRYING METHODS Press individual flowers in flower press or dry in desiccant.

Pernettya Prickly heath
Low shrubs with small bell shaped flowers, but it is the mass of round berries which clothe the stems that are most useful in arrangements. Available in a range of colours: white, pink and red. Evergreen.
AVAILABILITY Flowers: summer. Berries: autumn.
CONDITIONING (FRESH) Scrape, slit and recut stems and then stand in deep water for several hours.
PICKING FOR DRYING Summer.
DRYING METHODS Dry sprays of flowers in desiccant.

Peucedanum Hog's fennel
Flat heads of white, yellow or pink flowers.
AVAILABILITY Summer.
CONDITIONING (FRESH) Stand in deep water for several hours.
PICKING FOR DRYING Summer.
DRYING METHODS Air dry by hanging or preserve seed-heads by standing in glycerine.

Phaenocoma
Phaenocoma shrub
The flowers are a particularly vivid pink, stronger than both helipterum and helichrysum, both of which they resemble. They are set off by the tiny silver grey leaves.
AVAILABILITY Summer.
CONDITIONING (FRESH) Stand in deep water for several hours.
PICKING FOR DRYING Summer.
DRYING METHODS Air dry by hanging.

Phaseolus Bean
Climbing plants with white, red, purple or yellow, pea-like flowers. Not suitable for drying.
AVAILABILITY Summer, autumn.
CONDITIONING (FRESH) Stand in deep water for several hours.

Philadelphus Mock orange
Hardy shrubs with heavily scented white flowers. There are double-flowered and golden-leaved forms.

AVAILABILITY Summer.
CONDITIONING (FRESH) Remove most of the leaves. Scrape, slit and recut stems. Follow with boiling-water treatment and then stand in deep water for several hours.
PICKING FOR DRYING Summer.
DRYING METHODS Press individual flowers in flower press or dry in desiccant.

Phlomis **Jerusalem sage**

Whorls of yellow sage-like flowers with soft felty leaves. Leaves do not last very well. Pick just as the yellow flowers start to open.
AVAILABILITY Summer.
CONDITIONING (FRESH) Slit and recut stems and then stand in deep water for several hours.
PICKING FOR DRYING Summer.
DRYING METHODS Air dry by hanging.

Phlox

Tall border plants with large heads of brightly coloured flowers in white, blue, pink, red and mauve. Last well.
AVAILABILITY Summer.
CONDITIONING (FRESH) Slit and recut stems and then stand in deep water for several hours.
PICKING FOR DRYING Summer.
DRYING METHODS Press individual flowers in flower press.

Physalis **Cape gooseberry, Chinese lantern**

Bright orange paper lanterns enclosing the fruit make these plants decorative.
AVAILABILITY Autumn.
CONDITIONING (FRESH) Pick when orange begins to show. Remove leaves. Stand in deep water for several hours.
PICKING FOR DRYING Autumn.
DRYING METHODS Air dry by hanging.

Picea **Spruce**

Evergreen conifers used for their foliage, particularly as Christmas trees.

AVAILABILITY All year.
CONDITIONING (FRESH) Scrape, slit and recut stems and then stand in deep water for several hours.
PICKING FOR DRYING All year.
DRYING METHODS Air dry foliage in arrangements and separate cones in basket.

Pieris

Evergreen shrubs with masses of lily-of-the-valley flowers hanging in bunches. The shiny young foliage is red in spring. Not suitable for drying.
AVAILABILITY Spring.
CONDITIONING (FRESH) Scrape, slit and recut stems and then stand in deep water for several hours. Boiling-water treatment when young.

Pinus **Pine**

Evergreen conifers with needle-like leaves in bunches and cones. Good for winter arrangements.
AVAILABILITY All year.
CONDITIONING (FRESH) Scrape, slit and recut stems and then stand in deep water for several hours.
PICKING FOR DRYING Any time.
DRYING METHODS Air dry foliage in arrangements and separate cones in basket.

Pithocarpa **Miniature daisy**

These little white daisies are almost as delicate as gypsophila, but each flower has a more marked daisy shape. Very pretty and ideal for fresh, frothy arrangements.
AVAILABILITY Summer.
CONDITIONING (FRESH) Stand in deep water for several hours.
PICKING FOR DRYING Summer.
DRYING METHODS Air dry by hanging.

Pittosporum

Evergreen shrubs with useful shiny foliage. There are variegated and purple forms. Last well in water.
AVAILABILITY All year.

CONDITIONING (FRESH) Scrape, slit and recut stems and then stand in deep water for several hours.
PICKING FOR DRYING All year.
DRYING METHODS Preserve by standing in glycerine.

Platycodon **Balloon flower**

Called balloon flowers because of their interesting shape while in bud, when the flowers resemble inflated balloons. The flower itself is like a large open campanula in a rich blue. There are also white forms.
AVAILABILITY Summer.
CONDITIONING (FRESH) Boiling-water treatment and then stand in deep water for several hours.
PICKING FOR DRYING Summer.
DRYING METHODS Press open flowers in flower press or dry in desiccant.

Polemonium **Jacob's ladder**

Spikes of white or blue, saucer-shaped flowers.
AVAILABILITY Late spring and summer.
CONDITIONING (FRESH) Stand in deep water for several hours.
PICKING FOR DRYING Spring and summer.
DRYING METHODS Press flowers and leaves in flower press.

Polianthes **Tuberose**

White-flowered, bulbous plants with very strong scent.
AVAILABILITY Summer. All year from florists.
CONDITIONING (FRESH) Stand in deep water for several hours.
PICKING FOR DRYING Summer.
DRYING METHODS Dry individual flowers in desiccant.

Polygonatum **Solomon's seal**

Graceful arching stems with small white bells hanging below the outstretched leaves. Very cool appearance.
AVAILABILITY Spring and early summer.
CONDITIONING (FRESH) Stand in deep water for several hours.

PICKING FOR DRYING Spring.
DRYING METHODS Dry with desiccant, or preserve by standing in glycerine.

Polygonum Bistort, snakeweed
Small or medium stems of pink or red flowers. Still look good when they have turned brown. Last well in water.
AVAILABILITY Summer, autumn.
CONDITIONING (FRESH) Boiling-water treatment and then stand in deep water for several hours.
PICKING FOR DRYING Autumn.
DRYING METHODS Dry on plant.

Polystichum Shield fern
This evergreen fern is very finely divided and looks almost feather-like. The fronds are very attractive and look good when they are set amongst any other dried flowers.
AVAILABILITY Summer.
CONDITIONING (FRESH) Boiling-water treatment and then stand in deep water for several hours.
PICKING FOR DRYING Summer.
DRYING METHODS Press either between newspaper under carpet where there is no traffic or in flower press.

Populus Poplar
Deciduous trees or shrubs with shiny heart-shaped leaves. Silver and gold forms available. Flowers of no importance. Not suitable for drying.
AVAILABILITY Summer.
CONDITIONING (FRESH) Scrape, slit and recut stems and then stand in deep water for several hours. Boiling-water treatment when young.

Primula Auricula, cowslip, polyanthus, primrose
Short-stemmed flowers, the majority of which are yellow, but other bright colours, including blue and mauve, are available. Many varieties are fragrant.
AVAILABILITY Spring. Winter as pot plants.

CONDITIONING (FRESH) Stand in deep water for several hours.
PICKING FOR DRYING Spring.
DRYING METHODS Dry with desiccant, press in flower press or crystallize.

Protea
Tender shrubs with large flower-heads of differing shapes in red, pink, white, yellow, orange and purple. They last a very long time in water. For drying, pick just as the bud begins to open; a rubber band will prevent flower opening too much.
AVAILABILITY All year round from florists.
CONDITIONING (FRESH) Scrape, slit and recut stems and then stand in deep water for several hours.
PICKING FOR DRYING Summer.
DRYING METHODS Air dry by hanging.

Prunus Almond, cherry, nectarine, peach, plum
Trees or shrubs bearing pink or white blossom. Many varieties have double flowers. Some flower very early. Last a few days in water.
AVAILABILITY Mainly spring, but also winter.
CONDITIONING (FRESH) Scrape, slit and recut stems. Follow with boiling-water treatment when young and then stand in deep water for several hours.
PICKING FOR DRYING Spring.
DRYING METHODS Crystallize, press in flower press or dry in desiccant.

Pulmonaria Lungwort
Blue, purple, pink or red flowers on low-growing border plant. Some varieties have silver, variegated or spotted leaves.
AVAILABILITY Spring, but also some in winter.
CONDITIONING (FRESH) Stand in deep water for several hours.
PICKING FOR DRYING Spring.
DRYING METHODS Press flowers in flower press or crystallize.

Punica Pomegranate
A spherical fruit with a yellowish-red or brown skin.
AVAILABILITY Autumn from greengrocers.

Pyrethrum
Daisy-like flowers in bright colours: red, pink, and white. Feathery foliage. Last quite well in water.
AVAILABILITY Summer, autumn.
CONDITIONING (FRESH) Stand in deep water for several hours.
PICKING FOR DRYING Summer and autumn.
DRYING METHODS Press in flower press or dry in desiccant.

Pyrus Pear
Trees with attractive white blossom in spring, and yellow or green fruit in autumn. Not suitable for drying.
AVAILABILITY Blossom: spring. Fruit: autumn. All year from greengrocers.
CONDITIONING (FRESH) Scrape, slit and recut stems and then stand in deep water for several hours. Home-grown fruit lasts longer.

Quercus Pin oak
All oak leaves press well, either in summer when they are green or in the autumn, as they begin to change colour.
AVAILABILITY Spring to autumn.
CONDITIONING (FRESH) Scrape, slit and recut stems and then stand in deep water for several hours.
PICKING FOR DRYING Summer.
DRYING METHODS Press between newspaper under carpet where there is no traffic.

Ranunculus Buttercup
Apart from the native yellow varieties, there are many other larger, brightly coloured forms with double flowers.
AVAILABILITY Summer. Florists: most of the year.
CONDITIONING (FRESH) Stand in deep water for several hours.

PICKING FOR DRYING Early summer.
DRYING METHODS Dry with desiccant or air dry by hanging. Press single varieties in flower press.

Rheum Rhubarb
The young leaves of the culinary and ornamental rhubarbs can be used. The leaves are poisonous. Not suitable for drying.
AVAILABILITY Spring.
CONDITIONING (FRESH) Submerge whole leaf for a short time and then stand in deep water for several hours.

Rhododendron
A very large family of evergreen shrubs with attractive clusters of yellow, white, pink, red and purple flowers.
AVAILABILITY Winter to autumn.
CONDITIONING (FRESH) Scrape, slit and recut stems and then stand in deep water for several hours.
PICKING FOR DRYING Leaves: all year. Flowers: spring and summer.
DRYING METHODS Leaves: preserve leaves by standing in glycerine. Flowers: press individual flowers in flower press or dry in desiccant.

Ribes Flowering currant
Deciduous shrubs with hanging clusters of small, pink or red flowers and fresh, heavily veined leaves. Can be forced.
AVAILABILITY Spring.
CONDITIONING (FRESH) Scrape, slit and recut stems. Follow with boiling-water treatment when young and then stand in deep water for several hours.
PICKING FOR DRYING Spring.
DRYING METHODS Press leaves in flower press.

Rosa Rose
A very large family of shrubs and climbers with a good range of colours. Many are fragrant and the majority have thorny stems.

The wonderfully fragrant Hybrid tea roses air dry well when hung in a cool, dry, dark place. Single roses and double, old-fashioned roses must be dried with desiccants for best results. Pick all roses for drying before they are fully open.
AVAILABILITY Summer and autumn. Florists: all year.
CONDITIONING (FRESH) Best cut in bud when showing colour. Remove thorns and then stand in deep water for several hours.
PICKING FOR DRYING Summer.
DRYING METHODS Air dry by hanging, dry with desiccant or press petals in flower press.

Rosmarinus Rosemary
Evergreen shrubs with small needle-like, grey leaves which are fragrant when crushed. Pale blue flowers.
AVAILABILITY Foliage: all year. Flowers: summer and autumn.
CONDITIONING (FRESH) Slit and recut stems and then stand in deep water for several hours.
PICKING FOR DRYING All year.
DRYING METHODS Air dry by hanging or preserve by standing in glycerine.

Rubus Blackberry, bramble
Thorny rambling shrubs with mauve flowers and black berries, often both at the same time. Not suitable for drying.
AVAILABILITY Autumn.
CONDITIONING (FRESH) Scrape, slit and recut stems and then stand in deep water for several hours.

Rudbeckia Coneflower, black-eyed Susan
Bright yellow, orange and brown daisy-like flowers with long rough stems. Single or double. Last well in water. Not suitable for drying.
AVAILABILITY Late summer and autumn.
CONDITIONING (FRESH) Boiling-water treatment and then stand in deep water for several hours.

Ruscus Butcher's broom, box holly
Curious shrubs with modified stems that look like sharp-pointed leaves, the centre of which carry bright red berries after insignificant flowers.
AVAILABILITY Foliage: all year. Berries: autumn.
CONDITIONING (FRESH) Scrape, slit and recut stems and then stand in deep water for several hours.
PICKING FOR DRYING All year.
DRYING METHODS Air dry leaves by hanging or preserve by standing in glycerine.

Ruta Rue
Shrubby herbs with deeply cut, blue-grey leaves which are very aromatic. The flowers are yellow but not frequently used.
AVAILABILITY Summer, autumn.
CONDITIONING (FRESH) Slit and recut stems and then stand in deep water for several hours.
PICKING FOR DRYING All year.
DRYING METHODS Press leaves in flower press.

Saintpaulia African violet
Very popular house plants with dark green, furry leaves and blue or purple flowers on short stems. Last quite well in water.
AVAILABILITY All year.
CONDITIONING (FRESH) Stand in deep water for several hours.
PICKING FOR DRYING All year.
DRYING METHODS Press individual flowers in flower press.

Salix Willow, pussy willow
Trees and shrubs with variation in bark colour, which is useful during winter. The majority also bear interesting catkins which should be preserved before the yellow pollen appears.
AVAILABILITY Stems: winter. Catkins: late winter and spring. Foliage: spring to autumn.
CONDITIONING (FRESH) Scrape, slit and recut stems and then stand in deep water for several hours.

PICKING FOR DRYING All year.
DRYING METHODS Air dry foliage by hanging and preserve catkins by standing in glycerine.

Salvia Sage

Shrubs and herbaceous perennials with long spikes of blue or purple flowers. Foliage often aromatic. Last quite well in water. The cottagey variety 'Clary' dries well. *S. farinacea* looks like rich-coloured lavender when dried.
AVAILABILITY Summer, autumn.
CONDITIONING (FRESH) Stand in deep water for several hours.
PICKING FOR DRYING Summer.
DRYING METHODS Air dry by hanging.

Sambucus Elder

Deciduous shrubs with large flat-headed clusters of white flowers. Many have interesting foliage, which can be purple, golden or variegated. Some have very finely cut leaves.
AVAILABILITY Flowers: spring. Foliage: spring to autumn. Berries: autumn.
CONDITIONING (FRESH) Scrape, slit and recut stems. Follow with boiling-water treatment for young leaves and then stand in deep water for several hours.
PICKING FOR DRYING Summer.
DRYING METHODS Press leaves in flower press or under carpet between newspaper where there is no traffic.

Santolina Cotton lavender

Small evergreen shrubs with aromatic green or grey stems and foliage. Summer flowers are yellow but of little consequence. *S. neopolitana* is particularly good for drying.
AVAILABILITY All year.
CONDITIONING (FRESH) Scrape, slit and recut stems and then stand in deep water for several hours.
PICKING FOR DRYING Summer.
DRYING METHODS Air dry by hanging.

Scabiosa Scabious, pincushion flower

Blue, mauve, white or pale yellow disc-shaped flowers. There are double varieties available. Last quite well in water. The flowers shrink substantially when dried.
AVAILABILITY Summer.
CONDITIONING (FRESH) Stand in deep water for several hours.
PICKING FOR DRYING Summer and autumn.
DRYING METHODS Air dry by hanging or dry small mature flowers in desiccant.

Scilla Squill

Short-stemmed bulbs available with star-like flowers in blue, violet or white.
AVAILABILITY Spring.
CONDITIONING (FRESH) Stand in deep water for several hours.
PICKING FOR DRYING Spring.
DRYING METHODS Dry with desiccant or crystallize.

Sedum Stonecrop

Fleshy succulent plants with flat heads of red, pink or mauve. Smaller varieties are available with white or yellow flowers. Not suitable for drying.
AVAILABILITY Autumn.
CONDITIONING (FRESH) Stand in deep water for several hours.

Selaginella Club moss

This is a plant that looks good preserved in a glycerine solution to which green dye has been added to keep its natural, bright green colour. Club moss can be used as a base for arrangements or bunches can be used like foliage. Conditioning not necessary for fresh arrangements.
PICKING FOR DRYING All year.
DRYING METHODS Air dry in basket or box, or preserve in glycerine.

Senecio Ragwort, cineraria

Yellow daisy-like flowers with valuable green or grey foliage. *S. greyi* should be picked for drying well before the yellow flowers open, as it is the leaves and buds that are attractive when dried.
AVAILABILITY Summer.
CONDITIONING (FRESH) Slit and recut stems and then stand in deep water for several hours.
PICKING FOR DRYING Summer.
DRYING METHODS Air dry by hanging, or press individual leaves in flower press.

Silene Campion, pink cluster daisy, nodding catchfly

The delicate little pale pink flowers of this garden campion look very fresh when dried.
AVAILABILITY Summer.
CONDITIONING (FRESH) Stand in deep water for several hours.
PICKING FOR DRYING Summer.
DRYING METHODS Air dry by hanging or press flowers in flower press.

Skimmia

Evergreen shrubs with glossy leaves and clusters of long-lasting red berries. White, scented flowers. Last well in water. Not suitable for drying.
AVAILABILITY Foliage: all year. Flowers: spring. Berries: autumn to spring.
CONDITIONING (FRESH) Scrape, slit and recut stems and then stand in deep water for several hours.

Solidago Golden rod

Long-stemmed plants with fluffy, feathery yellow plumes. Last quite well in water. They can be dried well before the flowers open to use green or when flowers mature.
AVAILABILITY Summer, autumn.
CONDITIONING (FRESH) Stand in deep water for several hours.
PICKING FOR DRYING Summer to autumn.
DRYING METHODS Air dry by hanging.

Sorbus Mountain ash, rowan

Deciduous trees which are useful for the clusters of white flowers,

silvery foliage which has good autumn tints and orange, pink or white berries.
AVAILABILITY Flowers: spring. Foliage: summer or autumn. Berries: autumn.
CONDITIONING (FRESH) Scrape, slit and recut stems and then stand in deep water for several hours.
PICKING FOR DRYING Summer and autumn.
DRYING METHODS Press individual leaves in flower press.

Sphagnum **Sphagnum moss**
Invaluable as a base for many types of arrangement. Conditioning not necessary for fresh arrangements.
PICKING FOR DRYING Any time. Available from florists.
DRYING METHODS Air dry in basket or box.

Spiraea
Deciduous shrubs with masses of small white or pink flowers either in sprays or flat heads. There are variegated-leaved forms.
AVAILABILITY Spring.
CONDITIONING (FRESH) Scrape, slit and recut stems and then stand in deep water for several hours.
PICKING FOR DRYING Spring.
DRYING METHODS Dry flowers in desiccant.

Stachys **Lamb's ears**
Herbaceous plants with soft, felty, grey or silver leaves and pale pink flowers borne on tallish grey stems.
AVAILABILITY Summer, autumn.
CONDITIONING (FRESH) Stand in deep water for several hours, being careful not to wet foliage.
PICKING FOR DRYING Summer.
DRYING METHODS Leaves: air dry by hanging. Seed-heads: preserve by standing in glycerine.

Staphylea **Bladdernut**
Deciduous shrubs with clusters of white, scented flowers in summer followed by curious,

translucent seed capsules which seem to be inflated. Not suitable for drying.
AVAILABILITY Flowers: summer. Seed capsules: autumn.
CONDITIONING (FRESH) Scrape, slit and recut stems and then stand in deep water for several hours.

Stranvaesia
Semi-deciduous shrubs whose red leaves when they are about to fall contrast well with the green ones staying on the plant. This contrast is also helped by clusters of red berries. None is suitable for drying.
AVAILABILITY Autumn.
CONDITIONING (FRESH) Scrape, slit and recut stems and then stand in deep water for several hours.

Strelitzia **Bird of paradise flower**
Tender brightly coloured plants whose flower resembles the head of a bird with a bright, long-lasting orange crest. Not suitable for drying.
AVAILABILITY Spring. All year from florists.
CONDITIONING (FRESH) Stand in deep water for several hours.

Symphoricarpos **Snowberry**
Deciduous shrubs with insignificant pink flowers that produce white berries, which stay on the long naked stems. Not suitable for drying.
AVAILABILITY Autumn and winter.
CONDITIONING (FRESH) Scrape, slit and recut stems and then stand in deep water for several hours.

Syringa **Lilac**
Deciduous shrubs with large spikes of fragrant flowers in white and varying shades of mauve and purple.
AVAILABILITY Spring.
CONDITIONING (FRESH) Remove all leaves. Scrape, slit and recut stems. Follow with boiling-water

treatment and then stand in deep water for several hours.
PICKING FOR DRYING Spring.
DRYING METHODS Divide flowerheads into small sections and dry in desiccant.

Taxus **Yew**
Evergreen conifers with dark green, narrow leaves. Also attractive, sticky red fruit in autumn. Some think it unlucky if brought into the house. Lasts very well in water. Yew dries well without dropping and it can be used as foliage in all-year-round displays.
AVAILABILITY Foliage: all year.
CONDITIONING (FRESH) Scrape, slit and recut stems and then stand in deep water for several hours.
PICKING FOR DRYING All year.
DRYING METHODS As for fresh and then dry in arrangement or air dry by hanging or standing in container with a little water.

Thalictrum **Meadow rue**
Tall plants with sprays of fluffy, yellow, mauve or purple flowers. The delicate foliage is finely cut and can be green, grey-green or blue-green.
AVAILABILITY Summer.
CONDITIONING (FRESH) Boiling-water treatment if wilting and then stand in deep water for several hours.
PICKING FOR DRYING Summer.
DRYING METHODS Air dry by hanging, press flowers and leaves in flower press or dry flowers in desiccant.

Thymus **Thyme**
Dwarf shrubby herbs some of which are very fragrant, particularly if crushed. Pink, white, crimson, mauve or purple flowers on short stems.
AVAILABILITY Summer.
CONDITIONING (FRESH) Stand in deep water for several hours.
PICKING FOR DRYING Summer.
DRYING METHODS Air dry by hanging.

Tilia Lime
The colour of the seed sprays can be enhanced by adding rust-coloured dye to the glycerine solution to lend autumnal tints to the material.
AVAILABILITY Spring.
CONDITIONING (FRESH) Boiling-water treatment and then stand in deep water for several hours.
PICKING FOR DRYING Summer.
DRYING METHODS Air dry by hanging, or preserve seed-sprays by standing in glycerine.

Tillandsia Tumbleweed
This extraordinary plant looks like narrow grey hay. It makes a lace-like surround for posies and ropes and can also be used to cover frames and bases. Not suitable for fresh arrangements.
PICKING FOR DRYING Any time.
DRYING METHODS Air dry by hanging.

Tricyrtis Toad lily
Sprays of intriguing white, mauve or yellow flowers, with heavy purple spotting, on tall arching stems. Last well in water. Not suitable for drying.
AVAILABILITY Autumn.
CONDITIONING (FRESH) Stand in deep water for several hours.

Trollius Globe flower
Yellow or orange flower like a large, double buttercup.
AVAILABILITY Late spring and early summer.
CONDITIONING (FRESH) Boiling-water treatment and then stand in deep water for several hours.
PICKING FOR DRYING Autumn.
DRYING METHODS Press leaves in flower press and dry flowers in desiccant.

Tropaeolum Nasturtium
Annual climbing plants with vivid orange or red trumpets. More tender varieties need winter protection. Last well in water.
AVAILABILITY Summer, autumn.
CONDITIONING (FRESH) Stand in deep water for several hours.

PICKING FOR DRYING Summer and autumn.
DRYING METHODS Press individual leaves and flowers in flower press.

Tulipa Tulip
Familiar bulbous plants with brightly coloured chalices in a wide range of colours including near-black. Long lasting in water.
AVAILABILITY Spring and summer. Also winter from florists.
CONDITIONING (FRESH) Wrap stems in paper to keep straight and then stand in deep water for several hours.
PICKING FOR DRYING Spring.
DRYING METHODS Dry with desiccant or press petals in flower press.

Typha Bulrush, reedmace
Bulrushes must be picked just as the roll of seeds turns brown, and well before the column starts to break up and deposit its seeds. Spray the surface of the bulrush with lacquer to hold the seeds in position as it dries.
AVAILABILITY Summer.
CONDITIONING (FRESH) Stand in deep water for several hours.
PICKING FOR DRYING Summer.
DRYING METHODS Air dry by standing in container without water.

Verbena
A large range of annual and perennial plants mainly pink, mauve and purple. Some are short-stemmed but others are very tall (*V. bonariensis*). Some varieties are scented. Last very well in water.
AVAILABILITY Summer, autumn.
CONDITIONING (FRESH) Stand in deep water for several hours.
PICKING FOR DRYING Summer and autumn.
DRYING METHODS Press individual flowers in flower press.

Verticordia Feather flower, cauliflower morrison
The strong-shaped, large, flat corymbs of flowers, which dry easily, add an interesting texture to arrangements.
AVAILABILITY Summer.
CONDITIONING (FRESH) Slit and recut stems and then stand in deep water for several hours.
PICKING FOR DRYING Summer.
DRYING METHODS Air dry by hanging.

Viburnum
Evergreen and deciduous shrubs with white or pink flowers, often heavily scented. Not suitable for preserving.
AVAILABILITY Winter, spring and autumn.
CONDITIONING (FRESH) Remove all leaves of *V. opulus* (Guelder rose). Scrape, slit and recut stems and then stand in deep water for several hours. Boiling-water treatment for all viburnums when leaves are young or in flower.

Vinca Periwinkle
Evergreen trailing shrubs with blue, mauve or white flowers. *V. difformis* has white or pale blue flowers in mid-winter.
AVAILABILITY Winter, spring and summer.
CONDITIONING (FRESH) Stand in deep water for several hours.
PICKING FOR DRYING Winter to summer.
DRYING METHODS Press flowers in flower press or dry in desiccant.

Viola Pansy, viola, violet
Varying sizes of the well-known viola-shaped flowers in a wide range of colours. All are short-stemmed. Some varieties are fragrant, and are delicious to eat, in desserts and cakes, when crystallized.
AVAILABILITY Spring to autumn. Some pansies all year.
CONDITIONING (FRESH) Stand in deep water for several hours.
PICKING FOR DRYING Spring.
DRYING METHODS Press in flower press or crystallize.

Vitis Grape, vine

Can be used for the foliage, particularly with autumn colour, or for the fruit. Vine stems can be twisted together in lengths of about 1.2m (4ft) to form rustic wreaths. Bend into shape before stems dry.

AVAILABILITY Autumn.

CONDITIONING (FRESH) Foliage: boiling-water treatment and then stand in deep water for several hours. Fruit: avoid removing the bloom.

PICKING FOR DRYING Winter.

DRYING METHODS Air dry by standing in container in a little water or press autumnal leaves in flower press.

Xeranthemum
Common immortelle

The papery flowers of immortelle will dry on the plant, but they are delicate and often get damaged if dried in this way.

AVAILABILITY Summer.

CONDITIONING (FRESH) Stand in deep water for several hours.

PICKING FOR DRYING Summer.

DRYING METHODS Air dry by hanging.

Zantedeschia Arum lily, calla lily

Pure white, folded trumpets with a central spike. Large glossy leaves. Some people regard them as being funereal. Pink and yellow varieties also available. Not suitable for drying.

AVAILABILITY Spring and early summer.

CONDITIONING (FRESH) Stand in deep water for several hours.

Zea mays Corn-on-the-cob, Indian corn, maize, sweet corn

Grass with large leaves and large yellow seed-heads wrapped in green and topped with soft tassels. The 'Rainbow' variety produces a selection of small, different-coloured cobs which are not edible.

AVAILABILITY Autumn.

CONDITIONING (FRESH) If height required, push a stick into the base of seed-heads quickly because they dry out.

PICKING FOR DRYING Autumn.

DRYING METHODS Air dry by standing in container without water.

Zinnia

Very colourful annuals with large double, daisy-like flower-heads available in yellow, orange, red, purple, green or white. Last well in water.

AVAILABILITY Summer, autumn.

CONDITIONING (FRESH) Stand in deep water for several hours.

PICKING FOR DRYING Summer.

DRYING METHODS Dry with desiccant.

INDEX

Figures in italic refer to illustrations.

ACKNOWLEDGMENTS

Designers: Mick Keates, Hilary Krag
Editors: Mary Davies, Catherine Tilley
Illustrators: Will Giles, Sandra Pond
Studio: Del and Co
Typesetter: Bournetype, Bournemouth
Reproduction: Colourscan, Singapore

Dorling Kindersley
Managing editor: Jemima Dunne
Managing art editor: Derek Coombes
Editorial assistance: Candida Ross-Macdonald, Julia Harris-Voss
Design assistance: Mark Regardsoe
Production: Jeanette Graham

Photographic credits
All photography by Andreas Einsiedel and Stephen Hayward, except: p 10 Alex
Starkey/Country Life; pp 206/207 Tania Midgely